The Agile Manager's Guide To

BUILDING AND LEADING TEAMS

By Joseph T. Straub

Velocity Business Publishing
Bristol, Vermont USA

For Pat and Stacey

Velocity Business Publishing publishes authoritative works of the highest quality. It is not, however, in the business of offering professional, legal, or accounting advice. Each company has its own circumstances and needs, and state and national laws may differ with respect to issues affecting you. If you need legal or other advice pertaining to your situation, secure the services of a professional.

If you'd like additional copies of this book or a catalog of books in the Agile Manager Series™, please get in touch.

- **Write us:**
  Velocity Business Publishing, Inc.
  15 Main Street
  Bristol, VT 05443   USA

- **Call us:**
  1-888-805-8600 in North America (toll-free)
  1-802-453-6669 from all other countries

- **Fax us:**
  1-802-453-2164

- **E-mail us:**
  action@agilemanager.com

- **Visit our Web site:**
  www.agilemanager.com

The Web site contains much of interest to business people—tips and techniques, business news, links to valuable sites, and electronic versions of titles in the Agile Manager Series.

Contents

*I*ntroduction: Get the Benefits of Teamwork

Teamwork, teamwork, teamwork! Is it *really* that big a deal? In a nutshell, yes.

The word is inescapable, and the technique is indispensable in organizations of every type and kind. Management trends may come and go, but teamwork's here to stay. Just check any company Web site, job specification, or classified ad, and you'll find that employers demand team-oriented applicants at every level.

In fact, a few minutes of random Internet surfing around corporate and recruiting Web sites produced the following team-related qualifications. As you can see, those who aren't team players need not apply:

> All candidates need to possess problem-solving skills, adapt to a multidisciplinary team setting, and want to be a key member of a hard-working group utilizing leading-edge computer technology.

> You will be a key member of a team that designs products from research to production.

> Leadership and the ability to motivate with an enthusiastic teamwork approach are necessary.

> Must be a team player with good communication skills . . .

Our client . . . has an opening for a Group Manager to head their development team in maintaining a Unixware version and developing a new NT-based version of the product. You will head a team of 20–25 software developers.

Position requires a very self-motivated individual with strong team interpersonal skills.

If you like to be quick on your feet, or strive for the precision of making your mark, you are what our team is looking for. We will be at the start with you and cross the finish line together. If you'd like to join [our company] in a victory lap, we would like you to sign up.

Teams are almost universally accepted today as the best way for companies to improve productivity, make work more meaningful, give employees a sense of unity and belonging, and answer the challenges of global competition.

Team Defined

In their book *The Wisdom of Teams: Creating the High-Performance Organization* (Harvard Business School Press, 1993), Jon R. Katzenbach and Douglas K. Smith define a team as: "[A] small number of people with complementary skills who are committed to a common purpose, performance goals, and approach for which they hold themselves mutually accountable."

Let's put some meat on that bare-bones definition. In my view, an effective team is one whose members:

- Have a common goal that rallies their resources, energy, talents, and skills. They believe in what they're trying to do.
- Set their own objectives, instead of having them dictated by somebody outside the group.
- Agree on quality, quantity, cost, and time standards. Each member has both oars in the water and is pulling in the same direction.
- Develop guidelines for behavior and performance that are enforced through peer pressure. Team members keep each other in line.

What Makes Teamwork So Hot

Today's technology and work processes have done a lot to help teams flourish in offices and factories. Employees may not wear sports jerseys and meet in a huddle, but they have to synchronize their efforts and individual skills nevertheless. Business procedures have gotten pretty complex and interdependent in the last couple of decades. They're often too difficult for one person to handle successfully.

Other reasons for the growth of teamwork include:

Process/operational inefficiencies. Traditional methods of designing, engineering, and manufacturing superior-quality products haven't worked very well since the 1970s. Companies that subscribed to the Lone Ranger school of management found that critical departments—and even employees who worked in the same department—were often isolated from one another philosophically if not physically. Things could get really screwed up.

For example, management at motorcycle-maker Harley-Davidson found that the oil hole in one model of crankshaft was drilled straight. In another model it was drilled at an angle. Machine setup time to switch from one crankshaft to the other took hours.

Why the inefficiency? Because the engineers who had designed the parts hadn't bothered to get together and agree on a standard way to drill the holes. After they did, setup time was reduced to several minutes. Teamwork scores again!

Downsizings. Teamwork is, logically enough, a natural byproduct of downsizing, too. The need to do more with fewer middle managers has left companies with no choice except to switch to teamwork. It's now common for nonsupervisory employees to make decisions and collaborate on many tasks that were once delegated to mid-level managers.

Competition. Competition, especially from abroad, has pressured American companies to reduce the cycle time for developing and launching new products from a year or more to a matter of months. The result? More cross-functional teams and

Teamwork Triumphs

When Miller Brewing Company built its Trenton brewery, the plant was intended to be a model of teamwork from the very beginning.

More than thirty self-directed work teams of six to twenty-four members handle all the brewing, packaging, and distribution functions.

Teams have no permanent leaders, and each has five areas of responsibility: productivity/maintenance, personnel, administration, quality, and safety.

Teammates select representatives by consensus to monitor their performance in each of these areas and coordinate their work with other teams. Representatives serve terms of twelve to eighteen months and meet with their counterparts on other teams every two weeks. Members design a system of goals, measurements, and feedback devices for their team and use that system to monitor, coordinate, and improve their collective performance.

Labor-management harmony is orchestrated by continual interaction between Local 2308 of the United Auto Workers and plant officials. The two groups solve problems jointly, instead of trying to beat each other up.

How well has teamwork worked at Trenton? You be the judge.

During the plant's first four years, production rose from zero to a heady figure of more than seven million barrels of beer per year. The plant has installed eight fully operational beer and can lines, and a keg beer line that runs around the clock.

Its productivity? Reportedly 40 percent higher than any other brewery in the company.

greater employee interaction across departmental lines. Some businesses report that new-product development time has been cut by two-thirds.

Better use of human resources. Management also better appreciates how teamwork can unify the power of people. Teamwork unleashes their creativity, encourages synergy, and satisfies social needs.

Groups can define and solve problems more creatively. Teams are good for morale and motivation, too. People generally don't like to work in isolation. When teams really click, their members share a contagious feeling of camaraderie, unity, purpose, and identity. They enjoy a sense of achievement and personal worth ("I can see that I'm needed and appreciated").

As if this weren't enough, teams also help companies to:

- Encourage and foster participation from everyone. Employees have more opportunities to make meaningful contributions.
- Advance ideas of total quality management and continuous process improvement across all departmental boundaries.
- Respond faster to market conditions, problems, opportunities, and customers' demands and expectations.
- Make more decisions by consensus—which gives them widespread acceptance, support, and credibility.

Profile of a Successful Team

A solid team has a profile as rugged as that of Kirk Douglas or the distinguished gentlemen who grace Mt. Rushmore. Characteristics reflect:

Number. Ideally, teams should be limited to no more than twelve members. Fewer employees make for a more workable team, because the more people, the harder it will be for them to reach a consensus, agree on common goals, and develop a strong identity. Too many cooks . . . ah, you know the rest.

Diversity. The most powerful teams have members who contribute diverse and complementary skills, knowledge, viewpoints, and experience. These qualities foster synergy—the whole team can be greater than the sum of its individual members' abilities. But then, that's the idea with teamwork in the first place.

In fact, it's ideal when members bring multiple skills to the team's table. This lets them trade off tasks and assignments, enhance each other's productivity and job security, and enjoy some welcome variety. There's no compartmentalizing. Teammates who have multiple skills help to reduce overhead, too, because management doesn't have to hire as many specialists to do certain jobs.

Respect. Members demonstrate mutual respect and trust. They are committed to working together for the common good of the organization and each other. This attitude also enables them to resolve differences that arise among themselves. The best teams eventually function so well that they need little outside intervention or supervision.

Analysis. Members monitor, analyze, and critique their own performance objectively, settle conflicts through negotiation and compromise, and take corrective measures where necessary. They're dedicated to continuous improvement.

Relationships. The relationships and interaction among teammates wind each member's watch. The dynamics of the association satisfy needs for acceptance and esteem and enable each person to make meaningful contributions. Benefits extend in all directions; it's a win-win situation. No one's been had. No one is conned.

Rewards. Ideally, the reward system reinforces group accomplishments and makes individual recognition secondary to them. On successful teams, members share credit willingly. Their attitude is "It's everyone's job," not "That's not my job." Teammates back up and support each other voluntarily.

Entire jobs. Members work on projects or activities from start to finish. This gives the team a sense of closure and achievement.

Understand Team Roles

As this profile suggests, team members play multiple roles. Each pattern of behavior contributes something to the mechanics and dynamics of the team. Logically enough, individual members and the team as a group must work out these roles. Defining roles often explains how certain teammates behave with each other and relate to the team as a whole.

Task Roles. These are individual team-member assignments that help the team reach its goals, maintain and preserve its identity and reputation, and "get the job done."

Task roles might include, for example, completing a certain activity such as gathering data for, writing, or preparing statistics to accompany a report; making specific types of decisions; or coordinating certain activities with those of related teams. Task roles contribute to the team's success.

Maintenance Roles. These are behaviors that keep the team unified and moving forward: resolving conflicts, supporting and coordinating members' individual efforts, filling in for each other or taking up the slack when problems arise, challenging the team's decisions and direction, achieving consensus and compromise, and respecting teammates' diversity and individual differences—whether occupational or cultural.

Personal Roles. These are self-serving "what's-in-it-for-me" roles. They can be played out consciously or subconsciously. The list is probably endless, but here are a few common ones.

1. Gadfly. This person can provide beneficial aggravation and some healthy reality checks. Gadflies challenge complacency and the status quo.

2. Grandstander/egotist. This person relishes the spotlight and has trouble sacrificing personal recognition for group recognition.

3. Thinker. Thinkers enjoy a challenge. They turn issues upside down and inside out to better understand what makes them tick. They're valuable assets to any team.

4. Peacemaker. This person is a moderator who can help warring factions find common ground. Peacemakers tend to be objective and levelheaded.

5. Comedian. A comedian can be good for comic relief, but the team can't allow the class clown to run away with its meetings. The comedian's humor is refreshing as long as it doesn't get out of control.

6. Distracter. Distracters introduce irrelevant information or issues. They have trouble focusing on team's goals.

7. *Nitpicker.* Second cousin to the gadfly. Nitpickers can remind less-meticulous teammates of the need to pay attention to details.

8. *Dominator.* Has trouble seeing others' point of view. Often loud and overly aggressive, dominators have a "my way or the highway" attitude.

Get the Benefits

The jury is in. The verdict: Teams improve productivity and employee satisfaction in just about any work setting.

So how do you get these and the many other benefits just described? Keep reading. Showing you how to improve your operations through teamwork—or improve the teams you have—is what this book is all about.

We'll cover creating different kinds of teams for different purposes, leading teams and the all-important team meetings, managing conflicts among team members and keeping people satisfied, making decisions as a group, evaluating team performance, and a lot more.

Let's get started.

Chapter One

Create, Staff, And Lead the Right Team

"Coming together is a beginning. Keeping together is progress. Working together is success."

HENRY FORD

"Teams." Wanda spat the word out as if she'd almost swallowed a bug. "So the people I now direct will start telling me what to do?"

The Agile Manager laughed. "Hardly. But there will be some changes. And I don't know what they'll all be. Remember, I'm new to this, too."

Wanda maintained her sour look. "I bet we go back to business as usual in six months," she said.

"I doubt it. Murphy Technology and Axxor and PotentialTech have all been using a team structure for a couple of years and show no signs of retreating. Get used to the idea, Wanda. It should be fun. And people say that productivity can increase 15 or 20 percent the first year alone."

Wanda, looking unconvinced, said, "So it's the 'Product Development Action Team.' I wonder who gave it that name. And no doubt my title will change from 'manager of product development' to 'facilitator' or some other wuss word."

"Look," said the Agile Manager, "all I'm asking is that you give it a try. If you can't abide it, we'll give you something else to do."

That shook Wanda out of her funk. "OK," she said. "I get the message."

"Besides," said the Agile Manager, "I've already got a title picked out for you: chief wheel greaser. Of course, you can come up with something else and put it to the team for a vote."

They both laughed, and Wanda bustled out of the office whistling the fight song of her alma mater.

One of the earliest questions you and your team must answer is what kind of team you're going to be.

There are five general types of teams, and each one plays a different role and enjoys a different degree of autonomy. Top management will usually decide which category your team falls into. In some situations, you may have the latitude to decide for yourself. In any case, be aware that the nature of teamwork changes and often moves along a continuum. As time passes, for example, a team may metamorphose from an advisory capacity to a highly autonomous self-directed team.

1. **Troubleshooting, advisory, or problem-solving team.** These teams investigate and analyze problems or opportunities and recommend appropriate action to higher management. While often temporary and endowed with minimal autonomy, they are good for generating ideas in brainstorming fashion and soliciting participation from a broad base of employees.

A troubleshooting, advisory, or problem-solving team tends to have little authority. ("Check out this problem, opportunity, or situation and suggest what might be done.") Such a team could be formed by a department supervisor to investigate a sharp decline in productivity, repeated machine breakdowns, an abrupt increase in customer-service complaints, excessive scrap or rework, or an intermittent problem in a computer software program.

2. **Policy-making team.** These typically exist at the senior-

management level. Their pronouncements govern the work of an entire facility (or perhaps everyone in the whole company). It's worth noting, of course, that lower-level teams regularly make informal "policies" that control their members' conduct, output, goals, and other issues.

Best Tip

Use cross-functional teams to cut through red tape and coordinate work across departmental lines.

3. **Action team or task force.** These teams may be assembled by higher management to implement solutions to problems or launch new programs. They may also install new work processes and procedures or modify old ones to "reengineer" or "redesign" or "reinvent" the organization or some segment of it.

Like advisory teams, these teams may be temporary instead of ongoing and may operate for a year or longer. Members have certain skills or expertise that make them critical to the team's overall success. When the changes will be widespread, teammates will be drafted from each affected area to provide the necessary input and help ensure acceptance.

Action teams or task forces might be assembled to:

- Review, evaluate, and recommend the purchase of new office or production equipment. Upon delivery, team members would also oversee its installation, including rearranging the physical layout and work flow and coordinating the training program for operators.
- Improve an insurance company's claims-processing procedures to increase efficiency, reduce paperwork handling, and improve customer service.
- Revise customer-service policies and procedures in a department store.
- Suggest how merchandise might be stored and displayed more effectively in a supermarket or warehouse buying club.

An action team or task force tends to receive its "charter" from on high. Such teams have the blessing of higher management. Their authority is considerably greater than that of a troubleshooting team, whose authority is minimal.

These "can-do" teams might be responsible for making sure that a company's employment procedure doesn't violate the Americans with Disabilities Act, setting up a benchmarking program to compare current customer-service policies with those of leading competitors, teaching in-house trainers how to use state-of-the-art delivery systems, organizing a school-to-work program to recruit high-school graduates, or revamping the company's current early-retirement incentives program.

4. Cross-functional team. Cross-functional teams are often used to create an entirely new product (or model of product) or to redesign an existing product or process. Their assignments are complex, demanding input and involvement from various functional areas of the organization such as R&D, design, engineering, manufacturing, purchasing, and marketing.

These teams may have little formal supervision. Members account for their performance either to their respective department managers or to a product manager who heads up their group.

Cross-functional teams can offer a number of benefits, including:

- *Innovation.* Members have a unique blend of backgrounds, experience, and viewpoints that helps them think and act more creatively to solve complicated problems and simplify processes.
- *Streamlined communications.* The team has one point of contact who's responsible for providing information or announcing a decision.
- *Customer orientation.* Team members tend to devote their time, talents, and other resources to the primary goal of keeping customers satisfied.
- *Rapid response.* By cutting across organizational barriers and through red tape, cross-functional teams tend to get things done much faster than traditional work groups.

Teamwork Triumphs

Through the use of "world-class timing" teams, Ford Motor Company compressed the time required to get the present generation of Mustangs and certain other models to market in approximately three years.

Teammates on these cross-functional teams included designers, engineers, purchasing agents, marketing person nel, and others who worked at the same location and reported to a product manager instead of to the managers in charge of their respective functions.

---

5. Self-directed work team. These teams have extreme authority and autonomy. Their members are frequently cross-trained in multiple technical skills and have full responsibility to plan, organize, implement, and control their product or service from start to finish, whether it's a component, a subassembly, or the entire end product. Members do extensive internal monitoring and supervision and often coalesce into a cohesive unit with a strong group identity, esprit de corps, and work ethic.

Self-directed team leaders must wear many hats: coach, facilitator, mentor, scrounger, supporter, and liaison to management and to other teams. One thing team leaders in this situation are not: supervisor or director.

According to Dr. Darrel Ray, a self-directed work team authority with ODT, Inc.,

> Self-directed work teams [SDWTs] are not a panacea, but they provide the framework for essential corporate processes like JIT, TQM, empowerment, and continuous improvement. All of these are strong ingredients in any successful corporate strategy to compete in the next century. . . . With SDWTs . . . management either gets out of the way or kills the teams. There is no halfway point . . . it's like being a little pregnant. Once the ball is rolling and teams feel the power and productivity they can achieve without managers, it is hard to put that genie back in the bottle.

Cross-training is often essential for members of self-directed work teams, because they have a broad range of authority and responsibility.

For example, work teams in state-of-the-art manufacturing plants may be cross-trained not only to operate one another's equipment but also to service, adjust, and perform routine maintenance on the equipment. They may also fill in temporarily in the materials handling, packaging, or shipping departments during slack time.

Cross-training can be a savvy management move regardless of whether it's driven by teamwork. According to *Textile Rental Magazine*, management at a Cascade Uniform and Linen Service plant wanted to reduce costs and increase efficiency by cross-training employees to do other tasks during low production periods. Job descriptions were rewritten so that:

- Boiler operators were trained to maintain and repair other equipment when they weren't attending to boiler room responsibilities.
- Porters' jobs were eliminated by having equipment operators clean up their own work areas at the end of their shifts.
- Employees who packed and wrapped clean linens were trained for jobs in other areas in the morning, before the washroom and finishing areas produced enough work to keep them busy.

This cross-training helped the company to reduce its workforce by 140 employees (many left through attrition) while increasing its weekly production of clean linens.

Combine Team Types If Necessary

Whatever type of team structure you choose, keep in mind that teams may defy precise defining in the real world and often wear more than one hat. Management has lots of latitude about deciding which type of team should be used in a particular situation.

For example, a team could be a self-directed, cross-functional action team, depending on the job higher management wants it to do. Although it's easy to categorize teams for the sake of discussion, their activities may overlap and blend together in reality. That's part of their value.

Hire Good Team Players

Once you know what kind of team best suits your needs, it's time to staff it.

Team leaders, like college football coaches, are out to recruit the best talent available. This isn't to say that the decision is going to be totally theirs, however. Members of self-managed teams often recruit, interview, and select new employees themselves—or at least play a bit part in the process.

Details aside, though, you and/or your team should take these suggestions to heart when recruiting and hiring new team members:

1. While keeping in mind the requirements of the ADA, EEOC, and other U.S. laws and agencies, revise your job specifications to list skills, work habits, disposition, personality traits, and previous experience that are typical of team-oriented people as opposed to lone wolves, hermits, misanthropes, or egotists.

Likewise, rethink each job's duties and responsibilities and rewrite the job description to reflect your company's commitment to teamwork.

2. Evaluate extracurricular activities, previous work experience, and past job responsibilities to verify the person would be a positive addition to your team. These may include, for example, participating in team sports, belonging to various clubs, a record of work in other team-based organizations, and a series

Level of Team Autonomy				
Low				*High*
Advisory	Policy-making	Task force	Cross-functional	Self-directed

of positions that called for the applicant to coordinate, cooperate, and integrate his or her efforts with those of colleagues.

3. Ask personal references, former supervisors, and other relevant parties to evaluate the applicant's ability to work successfully as part of your team.

4. Discuss the job description with the applicant. Confirm that he or she feels comfortable with the position's team-related demands.

5. Assess the candidate's attitude toward teamwork by asking such questions as:

- "How do you feel about sharing recognition for your work with co-workers instead of getting the credit yourself?"
- "How comfortable are you in situations in which you have to depend on others to do your work and they, in turn, must depend on you?"
- "How would you respond to criticism from co-workers who weren't pleased with your behavior or performance?"
- "Let's say you seriously disagreed with a co-worker or had a personality conflict. How would you go about dealing with that?"

6. Include your team in the interview process. This gives both present teammates and the applicant an opportunity to size each other up and clarify their respective requirements, expectations, and feelings about working together. Teammates could also discuss their roles and responsibilities informally with the applicant to expand on and personalize the formal language in the job description.

7. Stress a teamwork theme throughout the orientation program.

- Give new hires flowcharts and other visual aids that show how teams relate to and interact with one another and how extensively teamwork is applied in your organization.
- Have present team members participate in orientation so new employees understand firsthand what co-workers expect from them.

Understand How Teams Evolve

Although teams don't emerge as slowly as do some species in Darwin's theory of evolution, management must be prepared to suffer some labor pains without the benefit of anesthetic. It takes time for team members to feel each other out (figuratively speaking), resolve their differences, clarify their respective roles, and achieve a sense of unity, identity, and common purpose. The process may take many months to work through.

Some researchers' views, like the photographs of Ansel Adams, have been praised and cited time and again for good reason: nobody has been able to come up with a better shot of the same scene.

That's true of psychologists Tuckman and Jensen—the Ansel Adamses of teamwork. Their view of how teams evolve has become a standard in the teamwork lexicon, and nobody's improved on

Best Tip

Involve team members in the hiring decision! Never force an applicant down their throats.

it yet. So we're not going to mess with their success.

Tuckman and Jensen identified four and sometimes five phases that teams go through.

Forming. Here teammates are on their best behavior—sort of like people on a first date or strangers in an elevator. They're tentative, polite, courteous, and concerned about stepping on each other's toes. No one's sure who's going to do what, how well qualified they are to do it, or whether it should even be done at all. Goals are unclear; relationships and responsibilities are vague.

Storming. Fireworks may go off at this stage as some members find, for example, that they both want to work on the same task or that they don't agree on goals. They may also argue about what direction to take, how to measure success, and the relative or perceived value of members' skills and what each can contribute to the group.

Storming is an uncomfortable period of adjustment. Eventually members' roles tend to become clarified and solidify. People debate, negotiate, and finally agree upon work assignments—hopefully without the use of dangerous weapons or threats of bodily harm. To apply the dating example, members have become familiar enough with each other to know their good and bad qualities, likes and dislikes, and things that get on each other's nerves.

Norming. This is a "cutting and fitting" stage in which members develop and accept standards of behavior that they're willing to be bound by and decide how they're going to do business as a team.

Norms or standards of behavior are critical to open communication and trust and necessary to minimize and settle members' interpersonal difficulties. Teams must eventually develop norms for the sake of team harmony and effectiveness.

Norms would apply, for example, to productivity, quality, cooperation, mutual support during rush periods, time management, setting priorities, resolving conflicts, making decisions, and reaching a consensus. Unlike dating couples, however, teammates usually don't have the option of calling the whole thing off and admitting that they would rather have a root canal than work side by side.

Best Tip

Expect fireworks and frustration at first, as team members iron out the wrinkles in their relationships.

Performing. Finally, the team is up and running and moving forward in the right direction. It's graduated from courtship to a solid marriage and is moving ahead smoothly. Members have cast off the old supervisor/subordinate "we have a boss" state of mind. The leader may fade into the background as the team embraces a collaborative mindset and an identity of its own.

Adjourning. Depending on their role, some teams may never adjourn. Like the Energizer rabbit, they just keep going and going. Action teams or task forces and some troubleshooting or problem-solving teams may be disbanded after they've met their goals and fulfilled their missions. If such is the case, management should congratulate the team on its work, throw an extravagant party in its honor, and call it quits.

Work teams are, of course, always evolving and changing—because they're made up of people. As members join or leave your team, it's likely that the chemistry will be thrown out of balance for a while. This may cause the team to revert to an earlier stage of development and cycle through the process once again.

Get Your Team on Track Quickly

In their jubilant reunion in the classic *Bonnie and Clyde*, brothers Clyde Barrow and Buck Barrow (Warren Beatty and Gene Hackman) whooped, hollered, pounded each other on the back, and jumped up and down. "We're gonna have ourselves a TIME!" shrieked one. Then, as they settled down and pondered their situation, the other asked, "Er . . . whut we gonna do?"

Such is the case with teams in general. They may set out to "have themselves a time," but it's important for team members to understand and agree on their roles, goals, relationships, and responsibilities at the outset. If they don't, they won't really know what they're going to do. They'll work at cross-purposes, duplicate each other's efforts, muddle around in confusion, and waste lots of valuable time and money. With any luck, however, they won't end up being shot like Bonnie, Clyde, and Buck.

Your goal, of course, is to get to the performing stage as quickly as you can. Here, then, is a team leader's readiness checklist to help you and your team get your ducks in a row. Answering these questions will keep you from flailing around like an octopus that's lost its powers of coordination.

1. What level of commitment does the team need from its members? (You must all be dedicated to specific, challenging, and realistic goals. A lukewarm or halfhearted commitment vir-

tually guarantees mediocre performance.)

2. Does each team member buy into the team's goals in spirit as well as with words? (Those who do not need specific attention and coaching. More on that later.)

3. What unique skills and talents does each member bring to the table? (List these on paper for each person.)

4. What lines of communication should be set up among individual team members and with other teams inside your organization? How about with internal and external "customers" these teams will serve or whose work they'll affect?

5. What internal and unofficial team-related policies and procedures will you need to work by? For example:

How will tasks be assigned to team members? By calling for volunteers? Majority vote? Consensus? It's important to rotate the most attractive jobs among all team members. Teammates will probably agree to that by consensus. Tasks that require specialized skills would typically require a majority vote to select the best-qualified candidate. Unpleasant work or jobs that depart from the team's normal routine, such as taking inventory, might be assigned by calling for volunteers.

How will disagreements and disputes among team members be resolved? Such disputes might be resolved by majority vote among team members, or, in the case of a deadlock, arbitrated by higher management.

Will work assignments be permanent or rotate among team members? Assignments can be rotated among teammates who are equally qualified to do them. This practice provides welcome variety and relieves boredom. It's likely, however, that teammates won't be cross-trained so thoroughly that they can handle anything and everything. In that case, some employees would be permanently responsible for certain tasks.

What method(s) will you use to evaluate the team's and individual members' performance? For example, teammates' individual and collective performance could be evaluated by the teammates themselves, with the aid of 360-degree feedback from both internal and external "customers," by higher management, or by a combination of these options.

What procedure will you use for selecting new members to join your team? New members may be selected by the team leader using input from the team; by the team itself, using the team leader (and perhaps one or more higher managers) as a sounding board; or by a consensus of the teammates themselves.

Plan to rotate both pleasant and unpleasant tasks among team members.

What methods will you use to provide information and feedback to team members on relevant issues and concerns? You can get team feedback by a host of methods, including information posted on bulletin boards and the company's intranet, team-wide or individual e-mail, periodic reports and team meetings, and informal watercooler discussions. Let the message dictate the medium.

How often will you meet? Who will set the agenda and make the necessary arrangements? You'll explore the whole issue of team meetings in chapter three.

How will you reward team members? Individually or as a group? A mixture of both? Sit tight for now. We'll get into that in chapter six.

6. Which customers (both internal and external) will your team serve most often? Should they have a role in evaluating the team's performance? If so, what might it be?

Who will answer the questions? It's also necessary, of course, to think about who's going to answer all these questions. Although higher management may want considerable input (you can't expect them to sit on the sidelines and twiddle their thumbs), you'll likely play a major role owing to your vantage point and the inherent objectivity of being a team leader.

Monitor Team Progress

Team leaders must be on the lookout for symptoms of trouble that may impair a team's performance and in some cases render it downright dysfunctional. These must be dealt with promptly if the team is to thrive and succeed.

- *Lack of purpose or goals.* Members may do productive work but their efforts aren't in synch and there's no collective sense of urgency, focus, progress, or direction.
- *Excessive bickering.* Conflicts are bound to happen in any joint venture. The key is to be alert to *excessive* disagreements and friction. Team leaders can't ignore team members who spend more time wrangling and sparring than collaborating on the work at hand. Lack of mutual respect among the members of a highly interdependent team can become contagious and catastrophically divisive.
- *Buck passing.* The larger the team, the more likelihood it will have some slackers, underachievers, and buck-passers who are content to let the rest of the team carry the load. Drones can't be allowed to kick back and watch other people work.
- *Mistrust of each other's motives.* This condition is often a carryover from the old politically inbred organization that teamwork was meant to put to rest. Team members who seem more committed to personal gain and glory than group goals alienate and polarize co-workers with their manipulation and self-serving maneuvers for high-profile assignments and competition for the limelight.
- *An inadequate mix of skills.* When team members lack one

Teamwork Triumphs

At The St. Paul Companies, self-managed teams in the Personal Insurance segment of the business have improved customer service in new policy processing. How? They've reduced the handoff points between the agent's office and the finished policy from a potential forty handoff points to less than twelve.

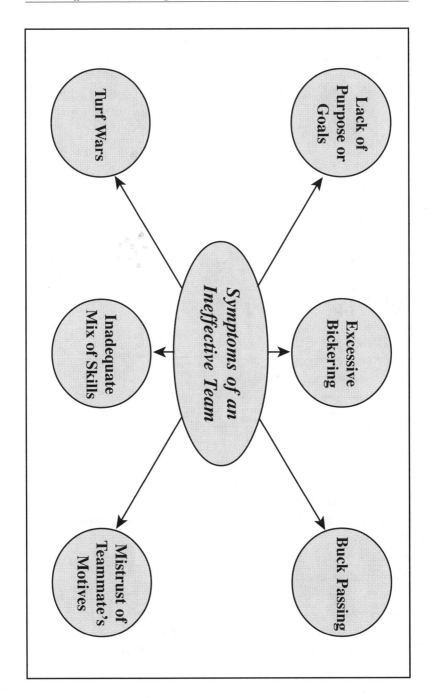

Turf Wars

Lack of Purpose or Goals

Inadequate Mix of Skills

Symptoms of an Ineffective Team

Excessive Bickering

Mistrust of Teammate's Motives

Buck Passing

or more skills that would ensure success, the entire group is destined to be less successful than if it had a full complement of the talents required to do the job. This is an inherent handicap that calls for either (a) recruiting additional members to eliminate the deficiency or (b) training to improve the existing members' skill sets ASAP.

■ *Turf wars.* Don't permit arguing over areas of responsibility or who does what. And don't let anyone object to cross-training and learning multiple tasks.

Span Boundaries

Good team leaders develop the resourcefulness and capacity to reach across the artificial barriers imposed by your organization chart. You do this to (1) obtain the resources and cooperation your team needs to function effectively and (2) unite your team's efforts with those of other teams both within your organization and inside suppliers' and customers' firms.

Best Tip

Support your requests for more resources with return-on-investment or cost/benefit figures.

Team members who know which key people to contact on other teams to get information, update the status of an order, or resolve a problem are in much greater control of their collective fate.

To span boundaries effectively and productively:

1. Organize regular meetings between your teammates and members of teams they work with regularly. Give your people the opportunity to discuss mutual problems, brainstorm solutions, exchange information, and generally build bridges and rapport with their counterparts.

2. Propose joint location. Cross-functional teams can benefit considerably having each function's representatives located together in a common site. This practice simplifies communication, unifies the team's purpose and strengthens its members' sense of unity and identity.

3. Assemble a team of team leaders. One of the most effective ways to communicate and work successfully with teams in other areas is to organize the leaders into a team of their own. The benefits?

- Higher team morale. Knowing that their leaders meet with each other routinely is a comfort to each team's members. They know that there's a channel of communication (the team of leaders) that can cut through red tape, expedite requests, and get quick answers to questions when necessary.
- Faster exchange of information. Team leaders who meet to trade information and assess progress on a regular basis will function more efficiently than leaders who only contact each other occasionally or when a problem comes up.
- Macroleadership. An established network of leaders that can get things done quickly liberates each leader to look at progress more objectively and be less obsessed with the nuts-and-bolts activities of leading their respective teams.

4. Know how to secure the goodwill of higher management and other teams. Effective boundary spanners can employ various strategies and tactics to secure the resources and cooperation they need from higher management and other teams. These include the following:

Construct a diagram or "teamwork organization chart" that puts the interdependent relationships among your team and other teams into sharp focus. This visual aid emphasizes the importance of spanning boundaries and maintaining mutually positive relationships with teams in other areas.

Justify your requests for resources from higher management in tangible, quantitative terms such as a cost/benefit analysis. ("Here's what my team needs to do this work, and here's the anticipated payoff.") Team leaders can't expect higher management to pay out more than a project or proposal is expected to bring in. That's a rule as old as business itself.

Make yourself a partner in your boss's success. Adopt a "we" orientation ("Our department . . ." "Our team . . ." "We need . . ." "We really ought to . . ."). This tactic makes it harder for him or her to refuse your requests for resources. After all, you're asking for tools that will help you polish your boss's reputation as well as your team's and your own.

Emphasize quid pro quo. Tactfully point out your willingness to reciprocate favors that other teams do for yours. Boundary spanners always remember that life is an exchange of services.

Make certain to acknowledge favors that others have done for you. Show your appreciation and remember your obligation to reciprocate.

Broadcast your team's achievements to higher management. Make sure your group gets proper credit and recognition. Proactively help major stakeholders by identifying needs your team can fulfill or problems it can solve. Emphasize the value of a mutually supportive relationship.

The Agile Manager's Checklist

✔ Decide, with your team, which of five general types of teams is most appropriate for your situation:

- Troubleshooting, advisory, or problem-solving
- Policy-making
- Action team or task force
- Cross-functional
- Self-directed

✔ Be aware that teams evolve through at least four phases: Forming, Storming, Norming, Performing, and (for temporary teams) Adjourning.

✔ Span boundaries both inside and outside the organization to obtain the resources and cooperation your team needs.

Chapter Two

*L*ead Your Team Effectively

"*Essential to teamwork is trust.*"

ROBERT H. WATERMAN
MANAGEMENT CONSULTANT AND WRITER

"Teams," said Manuel. "Yuck."

Shoe's on the other foot, Wanda thought uncomfortably. "Come on you guys," she said to the eight members of the Product Development Action Team late Friday afternoon. "All we're asking is that you give it a try. If you don't like it, we might be able to find another place for you somewhere in the company." Her stress on the word "might" got the group's attention.

"So what do we do next?" asked Anita.

"We'll have team training for two hours a day all next week," said Wanda. "After that, it's for you—us—to decide."

"Can we decide what to work on?"

"Maybe—if we get good at this," Wanda said brightly. "But senior management will mostly give us projects. They tell us the 'what,' and we figure out the 'how.'"

"So what's the 'what' this time?" asked Phil.

"Our job is to get the 3600A out the door by January 31 of next

year." A few people groaned; someone muttered, *"Sure thing."*

"And if you're not cracking the whip—I mean, if you're not directing us, what are you going to do?" asked Manuel with a smirk.

"Hey, I was an ace product developer myself, remember. At least half the time I'll be back in the trenches with you. The other half I'll be running interference—setting up meetings, getting us tools or money, coordinating with the manufacturing and marketing teams, and stuff like that. Just think of me as a giant oil can."

A few people laughed; Manuel tried to square that image with the view he usually took of Wanda—as a giant piece of sand paper.

"You all have a lot to think about," continued Wanda. *"Come in Monday ready for something new."*

The group dispersed without a word.

"Team leader." There's lots of responsibility (and perhaps a touch of anxiety) wrapped up in those two words. If you've just been anointed with that title, and you're not sure what to do, let's kick back and ponder your situation for a while.

Why People Resist Teamwork

Newly minted team leaders can be frustrated by the prospect of assembling a loosely knit work group into a legitimate, functioning team. This is especially true when your organization is just trying the concept on for size and everyone is working in a state of controlled confusion.

Be prepared for some opposition. Employees may not embrace teamwork with open arms for various reasons. Knowing what these reasons are helps you cope with them better. They include:

- *Reluctance to discard the traditional corporate culture.* Small wonder, really. Familiar ways and old habits are comfortable for most of us. They're predictable, warm and fuzzy. They don't hide any nasty surprises. Teamwork creates corporate culture shock.
- *Denial.* People don't like to admit that business practices

they worked hard to conceive and implement in the past and that were once state of the art may no longer be right for today's business environment. It's tough to acknowledge that things we invested so much time, effort, and commitment in have decreased in value. Doing so calls into question the wisdom of past decisions and the worth of former achievements.

- *Limited job advancement possibilities.* Opportunities for promotion may be fewer, because teamwork is usually the child of downsizing.

- *Group accomplishments taking precedence over individual achievements, recognition, and rewards.* People fear they'll lose their identity and become anonymous.

Personalities also get in the way of teamwork:

- *Old-school "I'm paid to think; you're paid to work" managers.* They don't want to relinquish control to teams. To them it seems like letting the inmates take over the asylum.

- *Top managers who may not want to share proprietary operating information with lower-level employees.* These employees, working in teams, may need it to set goals, establish priorities, and evaluate progress.

- *Workers who prefer the structure and limits of a traditional job.* Teamwork demands that they learn new work processes and human-relations skills.

Okay, so teamwork may go against the grain of workers and managers for some of the reasons mentioned above. That's understandable, but it shouldn't be used as an excuse for doing business as usual.

Teamwork has become an almost universal practice, as this book's introduction pointed out. And it's not going to go away. Sure, the idea won't be popular with employees in a traditional company, but they'll come to accept it once they see that you mean business—and that you and the managers above you believe the benefits far outweigh the effort to change to a team-based system.

Cultivate Leadership Qualities

No matter what your official job description says, team members and higher management will expect—and in some cases demand—that you honor certain expectations and cultivate the qualities of a sound team leader. Some are personal, others are professional, all are key ingredients in your recipe for success. Prepare yourself to:

- Communicate your organization's goals in terms that your teammates can understand and will support on a personal level. Effective team leaders sell employees on teamwork by showing them "what's in it for you."
- Establish your reputation as an evenhanded, people-oriented manager who's patient, level-headed, and reliable.
- Motivate employees to elevate group goals above personal goals and group rewards above individual rewards.
- Act as a champion of change.
- Be results-oriented, not methods-oriented. Effective team leaders provide general direction. They focus on *what* the team must do, not *how* it'll do it. The how, in fact, is often left up to team members to decide—and rightfully so.

Observe Your Team Closely

You may have suspected by now that a big part of your job is to be a process monitor and remote-control leader. Agile team leaders are adept at assessing how teammates relate to and interact with one another. They identify patterns of behavior that should be encouraged and nurtured. They also watch out for conduct that should be discouraged or eliminated because it impairs the team's effectiveness. Successful leaders constantly observe and analyze at least three aspects of their team.

1. Collective team needs. Assess your team's needs for direction, vision, guidance, authority, reassurance, recognition, and resources. Satisfy those needs as thoroughly as possible. You'll be called on to build communication bridges, tear down barriers, and facilitate interaction among the members of your team and enhance their relationships with other teams. You'll also have to lead your teammates to challenge both their opinions and their performance when they're reluctant to do so.

2. Individual member dynamics. Here you have to dig beneath the surface and analyze the forces that influence individual members of your team and make them tick. These include, for example:

Best Tip

Don't expect people to be enthusiastic about teamwork right away. Winning them over takes time.

- Key personality traits
- Experience and skills each member contributes to the team and training and development that would improve the value of each as team players
- Personal prejudices (which may be either positive or negative, depending on the person's nature)
- Rewards people hope to receive from team membership
- Needs for status and recognition
- Degree of commitment to the team's success
- Willingness to share their views and speak their minds, especially in the face of criticism and peer pressure.

3. The group's dynamics. Here you step back and look at the forest instead of the trees. While acknowledging the interplay of individual member dynamics, you also have to assess how teammates relate to the team as a unit. This calls for you to:

- Recognize major opinion leaders on your team
- Identify subgroups and factions that may favor or oppose the team's identity, unity, and goals
- Map channels of communication, patterns of influence, and informal alliances that arise among team members
- Assess the team's tolerance for minority viewpoints
- Identify interpersonal conflicts and turf wars among members who may pursue the same responsibilities or tasks
- Evaluate the team's ability to assess its work objectively and set challenging goals.

Teamwork Triumphs

Duke Energy Corporation (Charlotte, North Carolina) honors the achievements of its work teams with the company's Chairman's Award, the highest teamwork award offered by the company. Now in its fifth year, the award recognizes outstanding team accomplishment in the workplace.

In one recent year:

■ The six-member Coal Ash Management Team was honored for the increased utilization of coal ash—a byproduct of burning coal—to almost 30 percent above the national average. At one time, Duke sold only about 24 percent of its coal ash, which was bought by ready-mix concrete companies. In 1994, the team became involved in fill-material operations in the Carolinas and increased the sale of this material to almost 60 percent, which saved the company more than $3 million in disposal costs.

■ The fourteen-member Mainframe Replacement Project Team saved more than $1.5 million by replacing four room-sized mainframe computers with two smaller, more powerful state-of-the-art units. The conversion had no negative impact on company operations.

■ The ten-member Safe Practices Quality Improvement Project Team unified Duke's various safety programs into a comprehensive program that helped reduce safety incidents and increased productivity.

Each member of the three teams received ten shares of Duke Energy Corporation common stock, an engraved clock, and a certificate of recognition.

Employ These Guidelines for Success

Okay, so you have an idea of how people feel about teamwork, what your job description should be, and the importance of observing and analyzing your team from three perspectives. What guidelines should you follow to enhance your success?

Set clear, meaningful goals. Your team can't hit its targets blindfolded. Goals must be well-defined and sharply focused. Quantify them wherever possible—in dollars, percentages, or other values that can be verified and measured objectively.

But don't stop there. Make sure your team's goals are meaningful enough to motivate teammates to sacrifice some individual recognition for the sake of the group.

Involve your team in setting goals. That makes the goals *theirs*. They'll work harder to reach them.

"What's in it for us?" should seem at least as important and appealing as "What's in it for me?"

One sound technique for setting meaningful goals is to involve your team in writing them from the start. This common-sense practice makes the goals *theirs*, not someone else's. Teammates have a vested interested in what they've agreed to do and feel a personal stake in the outcome.

One final suggestion: Communicate and dramatize these goals so team members will appreciate the impact of their skills and effort.

For example, these goals might be:

- Reduce downtime for routine maintenance by 15 percent. This would enable us to make and sell 27,300 more units than last year and increase net income by $118,450.
- Cross-train each team member to perform at least one additional task within the department. This would qualify the team for a $20,000 bonus under the company's skill-development program.
- Redesign our Kamikaze Wombat motorcycle's suspension system to lower the center of gravity and increase stability at high speeds. This change should reduce the likelihood of accidents and product liability lawsuits by at least 25 percent and save the company at least $32 million in product liability insurance, out-of-court settlements, and legal de-

fense costs. That represents $2 million in savings for each person on our design team.

Build mutual trust. Trust, like interest, isn't paid in advance. It must be earned every day. You must convince your teammates that you won't sacrifice them to save your own hide and that they can rely on you and one another.

Trust also means that team members can count on you to share all news—good and bad—openly. They also need to know you won't shoot messengers who bear bad tidings.

Be patient. Teams and team leaders who resolve to conquer the world in a day (or a month, or six months) are usually doomed to fail, and the experience can be devastating and demoralizing. It's better to pursue small victories, gain momentum, bond as a unit, and move forward by the inch instead of the yard. Small successes build confidence, give your team a sense of progress, and encourage it to tackle more ambitious projects and take greater risks down the road.

Secure higher management support. One of the best ways to earn your teammates' respect and loyalty is to go to bat for them and become their biggest advocate with higher management. Lobby for teamwork orientation and training. Push for changes in policies, procedures, and work methods that would make them more "team friendly." Collaborate with teammates on physical work layout changes which, if approved by higher management, would simplify their communications and work flow.

Best Tip

Go to bat for your team. Become its biggest advocate with higher management. It'll earn team members' respect.

For example, management at one textile manufacturing plant decided to replace its fifty-year-old looms with state-of-the-art models made in Italy. A team of shift supervisors and top-performing production and mainte-nance workers was dispatched to Italy to learn how to set them up and perform maintenance and repairs. After returning, the

---

Teamwork Triumphs

Workers with interchangeable skills at Corning, Inc.'s Blacksburg, Virginia, plant have decreased the time required to retool a production line to make a different style of product from one hour to ten minutes.

Employees at this plant work 12½ hour shifts and alternate between three- and four-day work weeks. Employee discipline, if necessary, is handled by team members themselves. Members must learn three "families"—or groups—of skills within two years as a condition of employment.

---

team decided where to place the new looms on the production floor to be most accessible for maintenance personnel, quality assurance inspectors, and materials handlers who kept them supplied with raw yarn and removed the finished goods.

Management approved the plan, which improved productivity and proved to the workers that management respected their intelligence.

Secure team-oriented individual and group training. This is one cornerstone of teamwork's success. If your organization has just launched a team system, team members must have training in such areas as group goal-setting, problem solving, negotiating, analyzing and improving work processes, resolving interpersonal conflicts, evaluating group performance, achieving consensus decisions, and communication. Work closely with team members to identify such needs and assess how well they've been met.

Surrender control. This is infinitely easier said than done, but it's absolutely essential. If you've been a hands-on manager in the past, here are some suggestions to make letting go less painful.

- *Put some physical distance between you and your team.* This will help to keep you from breathing down their necks. For example, you might relocate your desk out of the main traffic pattern or set up a bookcase or portable partition to break the line of sight between you and your people. Remember, though, not to let physical barriers or distance discourage team members from approaching you or make you inaccessible.

■ *Ask a trusted colleague who has successfully made the transition from traditional supervisor to team leader to be your mentor.* This person should be willing to critique your behavior and point out incidents and conduct that are detrimental to team spirit. You, of course, must be willing to accept that person's criticism with an open mind.

■ *Announce your determination to let go.* Telling the members of your team that you've resolved to become less of a hands-on manager puts your pride on the line. They'll hold you to your pledge, and that provides added motivation for you to keep your word.

■ *Keep a contact log.* Record the number of times you just happened to "drop by" teammates' work areas, called them on the phone, e-mailed, or scheduled meetings. After you've accumulated several days worth of history, challenge the purpose of each incident. Which contacts were genuinely necessary? Which were basically meddling or kibitzing and therefore unnecessary? Identifying and categorizing your intrusive behavior is the first step toward justifying your contacts with teammates—and interrupting them only when absolutely necessary.

Set high performance standards. Part of your responsibility as a team leader is to pursue successively higher achievement over time. Like every good postal worker, you have to (ahem) push the envelope.

Challenge your team's comfort with the status quo and plant a few thorns in its laurels with such questions as:

1. How/where can we improve?
2. Why do we have to do it that way?
3. Who's got a better idea?
4. How is this being done in other benchmark organiza-

tions, in other departments, by other teams, etc.?

    5. Where aren't we working up to our full potential?

    6. Why can't we do better than this?

    7. What's holding us back?

    8. Why aren't we the best?

    9. Are we honestly challenging ourselves?

   10. Have we looked at this from every possible angle?

Pursue diversity. "Diversity" in this sense reaches far beyond the scope of its contemporary meaning. Leaders who pursue team diversity are committed to assembling people with diverse personalities, viewpoints, thought processes, backgrounds, training, education, and experience. In other words, put together a crazy-quilt of philosophies, priorities, and attitudes.

That kind of diversity can be the heart and soul of creative risk-taking and problem-solving. It ensures that you haven't assembled a bunch of group-think lemmings. Like-minded people won't rock the boat. They're weather vanes who'll point anywhere the wind blows them and will scurry for a safe harbor at the first sign of rough weather.

You, of course, are expected not only to accept but applaud your eclectic team's potential for constructive disagreement, dissent, and dispute—and its potential to be a font of creativity.

Keep an open mind. This is essential to assembling that team of diverse thinkers mentioned above. But there's more. You, as a team leader, must learn, learn, and learn! Listen to new ideas, no matter where they come from.

Use positive, teamwork-oriented language. Instead of "I" say "we"; instead of "your" say "our."

Nobody owns the patent on creativity. Make yourself a magnet for fresh ideas and offbeat viewpoints.

Develop a team-oriented vocabulary. When it comes to teamwork, your words reveal your attitude, feelings, and mindset at least as much as your actions. Team members will be quick to note, by what you say and how you say it, whether you're genuinely committed to a teamwork philosophy or merely paying it lip service. For example:

Traditional Management Language	Team Leader Language
I	We
Your	Our
I disagree	Have you considered . . .
You could have done better	We can all do better
What are you going to do?	What should we do?
I suggest . . .	What do you recommend?
Here's what I think	What's our consensus?
You should have done it differently	What should we do differently next time?
Is there anything I can do?	Tell me how I can help
You have a problem	We've got a problem

The Agile Manager's Checklist

✔ Expect people to resist a move to teamwork because of tradition, fear of losing control, fewer promotional opportunities, and lack of individual recognition.

✔ Live up to your teammates' personal and professional expectations.

✔ Your success will also hinge on your ability to:

- Set clear, meaningful team goals.
- Build mutual trust.
- Obtain higher management's support.
- Secure good training.
- Surrender control to your team.
- Challenge your team with high standards.
- Pursue diversity in assembling team members.

Chapter Three

Lead Productive Team Meetings

"The ratio of We's *to* I's *is the best indicator
of the development of a team."*

LEWIS D. EIGEN
EXECUTIVE VICE PRESIDENT, UNIVERSITY RESEARCH CORP.

"The meeting's objective is to figure out, in broad terms, how we're going to meet the deadline, Manuel. It's not about who's going to do what." Wanda pursed her lips so she wouldn't scowl at him.

"I understand that," said Manuel. "I can only answer that question if I know if I will have complete control over creating prototypes."

"Manuel," said Anita, "none of us will have 'complete control' over anything. That's why it's called a team. As I understand it, we'll all decide together which jobs we'll do." She looked at Wanda for confirmation. Wanda nodded.

Manuel looked genuinely confused and started to say something. He stopped.

"Say it, Manuel," Wanda said kindly. "Whatever it is. Let's get it on the table."

"Excuse me Wanda," said Phil. This month's sergeant-at-arms, Phil glared toward the end of the table toward two people whispering. "Anita and Will, can you save that for after the meeting? Thanks." They looked embarrassed and stopped talking.

"Manuel?" prompted Wanda.

"It's just that prototypes is what I'm best at. What if you all stick me somewhere else?"

"We know, I think, what each of us is best at. That's an advantage of teams—no pointy-headed bureaucrat can put us in the wrong job." The Agile Manager, leaning against the doorway, snickered. "In any case," continued Wanda, "you have a say, too, where you fit in. Nobody's going to put you in the wrong spot."

Manuel, relieved, said, "Well, I don't see any problem in getting the product out the door by January 31. All we have to do is make sure that . . ."

Meetings are important to work teams for a number of reasons.

- They give team members a sense of unity and purpose, which is especially important during the team's formative stages.
- They allow teammates to brainstorm ideas, exchange information, and relate to each other on a personal and professional level.
- They ensure that all team members receive the same information in the same fashion and can respond to it immediately if necessary.
- They keep all team members "in the loop" when disseminating information from outside sources.
- They give the team leader an opportunity to evaluate team members' roles and relationships as they interact with each other in the same room.

Unless there's a crisis or an emergency, try not to "call a meeting." It's your *team's* meeting. The people on it should play a central role in deciding when, where, and why they need to get together. You should wear the hats of facilitator, monitor, guide, evaluator, summarizer, and encourager—perhaps all at the same time.

Meet How Often?

Teams will need to meet more often in the early phases of their development than after they're up and running. It's important to have team members discuss how often they should meet. If your team is still in the Forming or Norming stages of development (recall chapter one), however, you may have to take the initiative by doing some discreet prompting or offering suggestions about meeting frequency. Be careful, though, not to strong-arm team members into scheduling meetings strictly to relieve your own anxiety.

If you have no idea how often to meet, start out with two or three meetings a week to establish the group's sense of unity and purpose, as mentioned. Meeting fairly often gives a newly formed team focus and direction and confirms management's resolve to make the group a team in spirit as well as in name.

Thereafter, meet only as necessary.

Create a Meeting Agenda

Teammates should collaborate on the meeting's agenda. They'll often need to explore issues or talk about concerns that you haven't considered or didn't know they were worried about. In addition, you should collectively decide on:

The meeting's objective. The agenda should cite at least one objective. Objectives provide a rationale for coming together and, it is hoped, confirm that the meeting won't waste teammates' time. A standard agenda form could be e-mailed or circulated among team members in advance so each person can indicate what information he or she wants to contribute to or receive from other members of the team. Some common objectives might be:

- Get a status report on the work of various teammates.
- Review problems and progress since your last meeting.
- Share information that team members need to make decisions and carry out their individual responsibilities.
- Define, discuss, and solve problems.

> ### Teamwork Triumphs
>
> South Central Counseling is a government agency that provides outpatient care, residential care, alcohol and drug counseling, therapeutic foster care, and a host of other services to ten counties in south-central Nebraska.
>
> After moving to self-directed work teams in 1992, the mental health professionals on the staff have celebrated consistent improvements in productivity and customer satisfaction at a cost that's generally lower than most service providers in the state. Teamwork has allowed South Central to improve its services, maintain level employment, reduce the number of people in management without layoffs, and share the gains with employees while saving on the overall budget.
>
> Teamwork's benefits have also enabled South Central to obtain additional funding despite times of tight money and fewer grants—which is an exceptional feat for any nonprofit service agency.

- Discuss, review, or rehash members' respective work assignments.
- Resolve conflicts that have sprung up among teammates.
- Brainstorm new opportunities or areas for improvement.

Resources you'll need and who's supposed to round them up. Expect to serve as a scrounger/facilitator who will scout an acceptable location, reserve a room, schedule audiovisual equipment, print the necessary documents, and arrange for key people to attend who aren't regular team members (such as higher managers, guest speakers, or experts who can supply information or insights that have an impact on the meeting's success).

Make sure to distribute the agenda far enough in advance so that team members can schedule the meeting on their calendars, assemble materials and information, and prepare themselves to participate in the meeting actively.

The scrounger/facilitator's job may, of course, be rotated

among team members so each one has the experience of getting all of a meeting's ducks in a row.

Prioritizing topics. Team members should decide which issues deserve the most time and attention and how they'll attack them. It's important for you, as leader, to play the analytical observer (recalling chapter two) and pick up on members' personal priorities and hidden agendas. Those who are too preoccupied with "what's in it for me" items can fragment discussion, frustrate progress, and impair the sense of accomplishment that people usually need to take away from a meeting.

Team members' meeting roles. Who will fill in as secretary, timekeeper, sergeant-at-arms, and other necessary roles? Consider rotating these jobs among all team members so that a handful of teammates won't gain higher status (either accidentally or on purpose) than their colleagues.

Operate with These Time-tested Guidelines

Team meetings can become Malfunction Junction without basic operating guidelines. These help the group deal with obstacles that would otherwise throw sand into the gears of a smooth-running discussion.

1. Consider developing, as a group, a standardized agenda for regular team meetings. This would list routine items that should be discussed at each gathering and allow time for new business issues to be discussed before you adjourn. Team members should collaborate on setting priorities for discussing new business items.

2. Don't let things get personal. Attack the problem, not the person. People who relish playing "the blame game," shooting the bad-news messenger, or conducting a witch hunt must change their behavior. Who may have caused the problem and why are questions best left for later. When the train jumps the track, it's more important for the crew to get it up and running as soon as possible—no matter who caused it to derail. Try posing such questions as:

- What should we do to fix the problem?

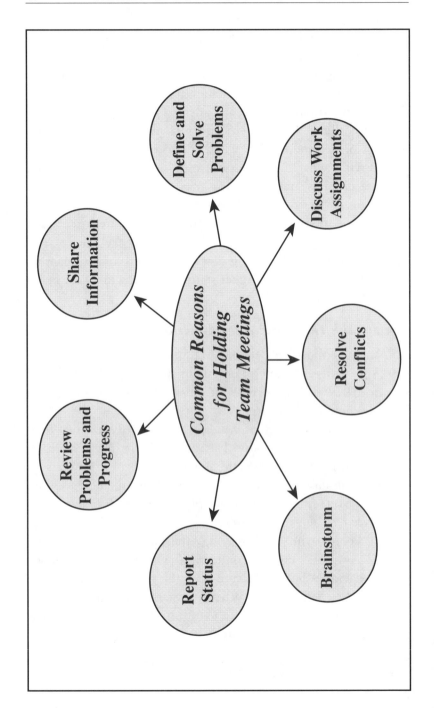

- Which of us is best qualified?
- Should we assign sub-teams of people with complementary skills who might collaborate to solve the problem faster?
- What should we do temporarily to prevent this from happening again until we can develop and implement a permanent fix?

3. Deal with teammates who hold the group oral hostage. One wry wit once commented, "It's all right to hold a conversation, but you should let go of it once in a while!"

Teammates who love the sound of their own voices can drag out meetings unnecessarily and bore the daylights out of their co-workers. Some teams use a common kitchen timer to keep discussion focused and regulated and discourage dominators and interrupters from monopolizing the conversation.

It's important to hear your more introverted teammates' comments and opinions, because these may often be modified and combined into exceptionally creative ideas. If you feel some members aren't participating because they feel inhibited by their more vocal colleagues, try to draw them out (and/or tone down the dominator) with comments or questions such as:

- "We need to hear from everyone in the room. Mike, let's hear your thoughts first, then let's have Stacey's opinion."
- "Frank, thanks for sharing your ideas about the problem. Now how about going around the table and hearing from everyone?"
- "Jean, you look like you've got some good ideas to contribute. Can we hear them?"

4. Suppress secondary discussions or "noise." In large groups it's common for two or more people who have no interest in the subject on the floor, or who need to transact business with each other, to strike up conversations among themselves. This distracts the team's attention from the subject at hand.

One way to discourage these distractions is to invest a sergeant-at-arms or monitor before each meeting starts with the authority to interrupt, nip these exchanges in the bud, and refocus everyone's attention on the business at hand. Rotate this position among all team members so one person doesn't end up labeled as warden or whip-cracking galley master.

Try giving your sergeant-at-arms a police whistle (which can be a real attention-getter) or just have the person rap on the table with a coffee mug when noise begins to get out of hand.

5. *Agree at the outset what measures to use to keep discussion moving forward.* For example, the group may agree to set a time limit for discussing major agenda items using that kitchen timer to sound the alarm when time runs out. If discussion on a particular item is deadlocked or spinning its wheels, the team might: (with some discreet prompting from you):

- Skip ahead to other items on the agenda and returning to that one later if there's time.
- Assign a subcommittee to gnaw on the bone of contention and report back to the entire team in a future meeting.
- Table the matter for now and call a future meeting specifically to discuss it (which would give people a chance to sort out their feelings, gather more information, and come prepared to address the issue head-on).
- Call a time-out for twenty minutes or so to allow everyone to take a mental break, gather their thoughts, and (it is hoped) gain a fresh perspective.
- Go around the table and ask members to summarize their feelings about the issue. Hearing what each other has to say in a nutshell can minimize or even eliminate some points of conflict and put the matter in sharper focus.

6. *Use subcommittees to deal with and report on agenda items that don't involve most of the team.* This practice doesn't tie up the whole group's time. Assign "experts" on your team to handle issues in which they have a vested interest, those that require specialized expertise, or concerns that will affect some team members more than others.

7. *Create and rotate the role of devil's advocate or "gadfly of the day."* This keeps one team member from feeling like an outcast

or catching all the heat. One of my former managers, who was out to exterminate yes-men, habitually asked different people in team meetings to shoot down an idea or criticize a proposal. ("George, tell me at least one thing that's wrong with this decision.""Ruby, this move is bound to have some hidden land mines. Tell me at least one.")

8. Be an active listener. Agile team leaders constantly observe and assess a meeting's progress and teammates' feelings using the following techniques:

- Make steady eye contact. If you want everyone to be involved, act as if you expect it. Looking team members in the eye lets them know that you're tuned in to the discussion and they should do likewise.
- Call members by name. This puts the discussion on a personal plane. You're talking *to* them, not *at* them.
- When someone makes vague comments ("In some departments . . .""I'm not sure . . .""According to the experts . . ." "Some people believe . . ."), ask them to provide specific details for the group's benefit. Which departments are you talking about? What is it that's bothering you? Who are these so-called experts? Which people think so and why?
- Challenge the direction of the meeting when it wanders off the topic with questions such as:
  —"Aren't we ignoring our agenda?"
  —"Is this something that we should assign to a subcommittee or table until later?"
  —"Is this the right time and place to discuss this?"
- Recalling the introduction, note which roles team members seem to be playing (gadfly, egotist, thinker, peacemaker, comedian, distracter, nitpicker, or dominator). Labeling their roles helps you develop a strategy for maximizing their value to the team and working out conflicts they may have with teammates effectively.

Active listening also pays dividends when it's necessary to summarize or redirect discussion, work for a consensus, highlight areas of agreement, and minimize areas of disagreement. You've tuned in to the discussion and followed it closely instead of allowing yourself to be a passive participant who's only partially aware of your team's concerns and dynamics.

9. Be a savvy questioner. The discreet use of questions—including your choice of words—may affect a meeting's productivity and success more than any other practice. Some key questioning techniques:

—Beware of leading questions. People often tend to answer questions the way they think the questioner wants them to. The trouble is, leading questions can inhibit creative thought and discourage honest opinions. For example:

"Don't you think that . . ."

"Aren't we supposed to . . ."

"Wouldn't it be best if . . ."

"Why don't you . . ."

Leading questions aren't always bad, however. A team leader who wants to exert some benevolent influence, redirect the team's thinking and direction, or encourage members to adopt another perspective can employ leading questions to do so. The point is not to phrase questions in ways that influence teammates' reactions unless you really intend to.

—Dig deeper. People in a group will sometimes indicate that they're harboring additional ideas, opinions, or information that they're reluctant to discuss openly. You can try to dig out these potential diamonds in the rough with a little oral spade work such as:

Best Tip
Justify your need for a meeting in a sentence or two—or don't hold one.

"How do you feel about . . ."

"Please tell us more . . ."

"That sounds interesting. What else can you tell us?"

—Pick up on "foundation comments." These remarks, which may be muttered under one's breath or dropped at the end of a

---

Teamwork Triumphs

Motorola, which has used teamwork extensively in most areas of the company for more than twenty years, credits the practice with reducing turnover by 25 percent, increasing productivity more than 30 percent, and raising employee attendance to 95 percent.

---

sentence, are often the tip of an important iceberg. People sometimes throw them out as bait to see if you really care about their opinions. When you hear them, follow up by digging deeper using some of the probing questions listed above. Typical foundation comments include:

"I could say more, but . . ."

"You probably don't want to hear . . ."

"I doubt if anybody cares."

"It's probably a waste of time to talk about . . ."

"That's just my opinion . . ."

"The decision's probably already been made."

—Read body language. Agile team leaders are fluent interpreters of body language. It accompanies many of the questions and comments mentioned above and communicates a great deal about someone's feelings. Nonverbal body language clues and cues include:

- *Eye contact.* People with strong convictions who believe in what they're saying tend to look you straight in the eye (life insurance salespeople, for example, but let's not get into *that*). Folks who feel ill at ease or aren't telling the whole truth often shift their eyes, doodle on a memo pad, or study their shoes, the desk top, or the wall behind you while they're talking.

- *Arm position and body attitude.* People who disagree with you may say so symbolically by crossing their arms over their chests. They're shutting you out and not buying a word of whatever you're saying. On the other hand, people who are enthusiastic or supportive may gesture animatedly or clasp their hands on the desk. Someone who leans back in a chair (often with crossed arms and legs) sends off loud negative vibrations, while listeners who lean forward with open arms signal positive thoughts.

- *Facial expressions and movements.* These responses tend to punctuate the "vocabulary" of eye contact, arm position, and body attitude. They can be positive or negative, depending on the subject. Look for such things as cynical smiles ("I am deeply impressed with your ability to throw the bull," "That's the most ridiculous thing I've ever heard," "You must be crazy!") or raised eyebrows ("I'm surprised," "I'm impressed," "Oh, really?" "I hadn't thought of that").

10. Consider using brainstorming. Team leaders who are agile brainstorming facilitators help their teams reach the pinnacle of their collective creativity. Some major guidelines:

—Set a time limit on the session. Original thinking, even in groups, can be exhausting. It helps to have the team agree on how long the session will run. Don't arbitrarily end the session, of course, when ideas are flowing in an avalanche and the group's on a roll.

—Tape record the meeting. This ensures that everyone's input gets logged. Besides, saddling one team member with the job of taking notes screens that person out of the process and denies everyone the benefit of his or her participation.

Best Tip

Remember: Some of the best insights come from people who speak the least. Encourage them to talk.

—Use artificial stimulants. These aren't necessarily sold by the drink! They might include, for example, popular magazines or mail-order catalogs, the yellow pages of the phone book, a dictionary, or other material that team members could browse through to help trigger free-association and uninhibited thinking.

—Leave the office. Offices are the world's worst place to think creatively. All they do is remind people about what needs to be done, hasn't been done, is past due, or is looming on the horizon like a funnel cloud. Get out of there! Go to some neutral or totally offbeat location. Rent a van and drive down the beach together, rent a meeting room at a local resort, stroll through an airport or shopping mall, go to an amusement park. In other words, put yourselves in places that will help you mentally disconnect from the daily grind.

—Ban criticism. Governments in some countries permit people who make critical comments to be shot. But that's a little extreme (not to mention loud and messy). Besides, where would you hide the bodies? Perhaps it's better for your team to agree on some token penalty. For example, negative commentators may have to put $5 in the kitty, which should help them redirect their thinking after they've paid up two or three times. One team armed members with water pistols and "executed" anyone who made critical or skeptical comments. So maybe we're moving closer to mayhem after all.

Best Tip

Use questions to guide, direct, challenge, and probe. And don't forget: Body language can speak louder than words.

11. Wrap things up effectively. Sometimes it seems that the only agreement that comes out of a meeting is an agreement to hold another meeting. Don't let that happen to your team. Productive meetings tend to employ one or a combination of adjournment techniques that leave everyone with a sense that they've accomplished something and received a meaningful return on the time they invested.

- Ask "Have we done what we meant to do?" If not, why not? What should be done next?
- Have at least two team members summarize what you've decided. Listen for discrepancies or conflicts in each version and iron out inconsistencies.

■ Ask team members to list the things they've agreed to do as a result of the meeting and when the work is supposed to be done. Teammates who need to work together on assignments should acknowledge that and arrange to do so privately.

■ Consider using a round-robin survey. One of my former managers, determined to get input from everyone, always went around the table and asked each of us by name: "_____, what else should we talk about that we haven't mentioned?"

■ If the meeting was called to reach a consensus, confirm that everyone does in fact agree. After a roller-coaster two-day session of contract meetings with a textbook publisher, the editor, a coauthor, and I all believed we'd reached an accord. Leaving nothing to doubt, the editor simply asked, "Do we have an agreement?" That was the litmus test.

■ Distribute the meeting's minutes ASAP, before memories grow stale and team members get too caught up in their work to read them and make any corrections.

The Agile Manager's Checklist

✔ Plan to meet more often in the early stages of your team's development.

✔ Ensure everyone on your team has input to the meeting's agenda.

✔ Don't let a few team members monopolize the discussion.

✔ Attack problems, not those who may have caused them.

✔ Select a devil's advocate to argue against the majority's position.

✔ Adjourn the meeting in a way that provides a sense of direction and accomplishment.

Chapter Four

Manage Conflict Sensibly

"The hammers must be swung in cadence when more than one is hammering the iron."

GIORDANO BRUNO
ITALIAN PHILOSOPHER AND ASTRONOMER

"If I did it that way," said Phil with a tone oozing contempt, "I'd burn out the fan in about two seconds."

"You wouldn't," said Will, his voice rising, "Not if you—" Will suddenly turned and stalked to where Wanda was watching and just stood there. She thought, this is the third time in two days.

"Come on, you two," she said. "Into the red room." That was the small conference room.

Phil rose reluctantly and followed them in.

"Phil," said Wanda. "What's the problem?" She tried to connect with the eyes he hid behind old-fashioned thick lenses.

Phil ignored her, looked at William, and said, "Do you need me to explain the nature of electrical current to you?"

You can be so mean sometimes, thought Wanda. She said, "Phil, I once wanted to know the 'right' way to design a circuit. My boss said, 'Wanda, there are a thousand ways to design a circuit.

57

All of them right.' What an eye-opener that was for me."

Phil considered this and said, "But there are probably only five or six that are truly elegant."

"Who's gonna see the damn thing or care?" sputtered William. "What's the difference as long as it works?"

"It makes a lot of difference!" Phil said vehemently. "It's the difference between art and mediocrity!"

"I suggest you two debate this over a pitcher of beer this afternoon," interjected Wanda. "Phil, William is an excellent engineer, and you know it. If it weren't for him, we wouldn't have had a crack at developing the 3600A. You know that, too."

Phil hunched down. "I'm sorry, Will," he said suddenly.

Wanda asked, "Will, can you explain your approach for us? I'd really like to hear it."

"Well, you take the red wire coming from the . . ."

Conflict is inevitable among the members of any work group. It can develop between two teammates, two factions within a team, or one person and everyone else on the team. Agile managers prepare themselves to manage and channel conflict effectively for the benefit of their teams and their careers.

Know the Sources of Conflict

Friction springs from various sources:

Lip service to teamwork. Don't be surprised if some workers don't support the idea of teamwork at the beginning. Although they say the right things and go through the motions, their heart's not in it. You can tell how they feel. So can the rest of your team.

If teamwork is the order of the day, everyone must buy into it. Lone Rangers with negative or halfhearted attitudes will contaminate and handicap the performance of the entire group.

Inertia. Employees who have worked together as a team for a long time may hate to challenge their group's inertia and a status quo that they've come to know and love. They don't want to rock the boat or upset their collective identity and cohesiveness. Their motto might be, "If it works, why fix it?"

Higher management probably won't allow a team to run on

cruise control for long. Challenging past achievements is more the rule than the exception in team-based organizations and standard operating procedure for those who relish the pursuit of excellence.

Cheerleaders. These folks are happy to kick back and applaud the efforts of their teammates while doing as little as possible themselves. If you look past their enthusiastic praise, however, you'll find they're simply slackers who aren't pulling their weight. These affable phonies can generate loads of contempt from teammates who resent carrying part of their load, too.

Best Tip

Beware of "cheerleaders" — those who clap loud for you so you don't notice how little they are doing.

A number of years ago I was asked to salvage a book project by rewriting what the original author had done, writing the remainder of the manuscript, and seeing it through to completion—with active support and involvement from my alleged partner. This match proved to be a shotgun wedding. The other guy was an expert cheerleader ("Great job! I really love your work! If only I'd thought of that! How do you do it?").

It didn't take long to realize, however, that he intended to bail out of the project as soon as I joined the team. Refusing to be taken advantage of, I insisted on—and received—control of the book and the lion's share of the benefits. I've been leery of cheerleaders ever since.

Cheerleaders are often found on larger teams, where they can coast without their co-workers catching on too soon. If not challenged, however, they can destroy the balance of the team's compensation program along with morale.

According to *The Wall Street Journal*, Unisys Corporation addresses the team-pay issue by having each member's performance evaluated by a team coach and three co-workers of the team member's choice. Compaq, too, has acknowledged the negative impact that cheerleaders may make on team compensation, but has reported no difficulties.

In addition to posing compensation dilemmas, there's also the danger that the coasters' attitudes will spread to the team's most productive members, causing them to throw up their hands and say, "Why should we work any harder than they do?"

Inequity. People have a keen sense of fairness. Expect them to make "equity checks" to assess how fairly they're rewarded in comparison to their teammates and counterparts in other organizations.

What will workers examine? Inputs (what they bring to the team) and outputs (what they get out of it). Pay is naturally a major output, but workers also place a high value on such factors as the nature of work assignments, the quality of their office furniture, desktop computers, reserved parking spaces, fringe benefits, bonuses, and other "goodies" that management seems to dole out with some degree of discretion.

Equity has three states:

1. In balance. Teammates believe that their efforts equal the fruits of their labors, and they feel content. ("Everything's cool.")

2. Imbalanced inputs. Teammates believe that what they contribute to the team (such as education, skill, and experience) outweighs the rewards they get from team membership. They may respond by reducing their inputs (taking long breaks or lunch periods, sneaking away early to play golf, or goofing off) or trying to increase the outputs (looking for a team or a job that offers better pay or benefits).

Teammates who believe they're giving more than they're getting will see no reason to work hard if their teammates don't. The workers will feel angry because they have to share the rewards with the drones and will chafe at the lack of individual recognition. Why should they bust their butts when no one seems to notice or care?

3. Imbalanced outputs. Teammates feel they're getting more than they're giving. This may cause those with a strong sense of conscience to feel guilty. This is, of course, a rare situation!

Arguments among teammates. The definition of an "argu-

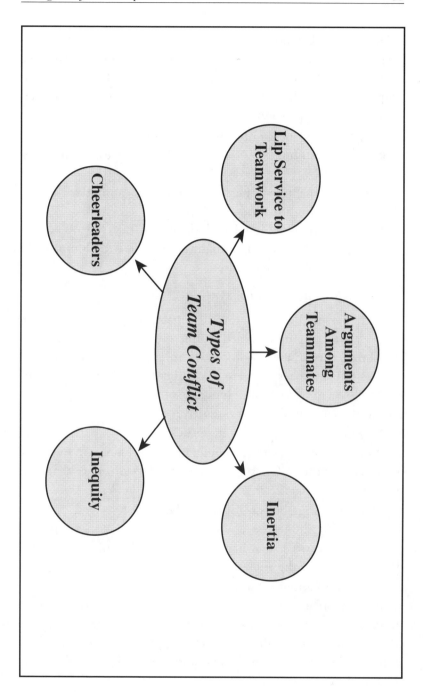

ment" has rubber boundaries that may stretch from a testy exchange of words to a screaming, wall-kicking rage accompanied by threats to "go postal." It's important for you, the team leader, to put these conflicts in perspective and assess their seriousness by asking such questions as:

- Is the problem significant and/or ongoing?
- How often and how intensely do these teammates cross swords?
- Do personalities or personal prejudices camouflage or distort the issues behind the disputes?
- Does the conflict involve work assignments, processes, policies, or procedures that might be modified to eliminate the problem altogether?

Promote the Right Attitude

Your personal attitude toward settling disputes affects your success with helping troubled teammates. In addition to understanding yourself, it's also necessary to analyze and label the attitudes of teammates who are in conflict before you try to bring them closer to agreement. Here are some common negative attitudes toward conflict and a positive spin on each.

Negative: My way or the highway.

Positive: We're creative, intelligent people who are expected to work together. We should be able to develop more than one way to tackle this issue.

Negative: Somebody's got to be the loser.

Positive: It should be possible to come up with a win-win solution if we work at it hard enough. Neither of us has to get the short end of the stick.

Negative: Compromise is a sign of weakness.

Positive: If history has taught us anything, it's that compromise is a sign of maturity and wisdom. If neither of us is willing to consider a compromise, this battle is going to drag on indefinitely, make both of us miserable, and jeopardize our productivity—and perhaps our jobs.

Negative: The first one who blinks loses.

Positive: We're in this together. If we behave like adversaries and attack each other like rabid pit bulls, we decrease the odds of resolving the conflict. How can we hope to work constructively if we've angered and alienated each other?

During my time in aerospace, I saw this toxic "hit him first and hit him harder" attitude produce profanity-laden shouting matches between so-called professionals that bordered on physical violence.

One employee got himself so emotionally psyched for the day's swivel-chair battles that he opened fire on an errant motorist with a handgun while driving to work one morning. Two co-workers who resurrected the previous day's argument in the parking lot the next morning got into a fist fight and were both fired. (It came as no surprise that this company had a higher employee death rate by heart attack than any other company in the industry.)

Best Tip

Expect people to make regular "equity checks" to compare their rewards and compensation with those of others.

Negative: You're pig-headed if you think that way.

Positive: Why do you think that way? What caused you to take that position? Have you considered [option A] or examined the validity of my opinion?

Negative: I have more education/experience/years than you, therefore I must be right.

Positive: We can all have good ideas, no matter what our background. Let a thousand flowers bloom.

Some people let their superior education, experience, or seniority stunt their imagination, short-circuit their search for better methods, blindfold their thinking, and truncate their success. Such an attitude can be professionally and personally catastrophic; it locks the door of a closed mind.

Agile managers are also humble managers. They refuse to in-

Teamwork Triumphs

Ashton Photo, the largest-volume photo printer in the state of Oregon, processes approximately 25,000 negatives per week from around the world. The company's strategy for success revolves around self-managed work teams. These teams answer directly to customers and are responsible for training, personnel and production decisions, and setting their own work schedules.

Since Ashton changed to a team-based management structure in 1985, worker productivity has increased 60 percent and continues to rise an average of 7.5 to 8 percent per year.

Sixteen teams, made up of up to nine persons each, are accountable directly to customers for all the photographs they print, package, and ship. Each of the company's three major product lines has a divisional manager who supports the teams in handling product orders and serves as a "barrier buster" to resolve issues that come up in weekly obstacle meetings. Employee evaluations are team-based. Employees who don't have strong support from their peers aren't likely to receive a raise.

Ashton posts weekly financial statements outside the employee lunchroom, and teams also receive profit-and-loss reports on their output from the previous week.

Ashton's work force is subject to seasonal reductions due to fluctuating demand in the photo industry. Employment at the company can range from a minimum of 90 to a maximum of 160 workers. Seasonal layoffs are primarily based on employees' accumulated skills, not seniority. Individual team leaders rank employees according to skill, experience, and the ability to work in a team environment. These rankings are then used to select workers for layoffs.

---

flate the value of their own opinions or take themselves too seriously. When dealing with others of this mindset, they break the intellectual log jam with such questions and comments as:

1. We should realize that there's more than one way to look at this situation.

2. Does anyone here really believe he/she is the ultimate expert?

3. Let's not let our education get in the way of our progress.

4. Let's not set up a caste system. We can't afford to rule out ideas from any source.

A motorist had a flat tire on a street near a playground. While putting on the spare, he lost the lug nuts down a sewer drain. "Now I've got to call a wrecker!" he complained aloud. A little boy standing just inside the fence said, "No you don't. Just use one nut from each of the other three wheels to hold your spare on until you get to a service station."

"How could somebody your age have an idea like that?" the driver asked. The boy replied, "Just because I'm only in second grade doesn't mean I'm stupid."

Deal with the Conflict at Hand

Conflicts virtually never resolve themselves. Like a virus, they usually grow stronger and spread to infect other members of the team. Don't ignore them or hope they'll go away. Attack them aggressively with a positive "We're all in this together" attitude.

Once you've analyzed (and perhaps revamped) your own attitude toward handling conflicts, turn your attention to the one at hand.

Begin by asking the parties to define and agree on the cause of their conflict. They can't collaborate on a solution until they share a common definition. Simply agreeing on the cause will minimize or eliminate friction caused by differences in perception. The next step, logically enough, is for the parties to agree that they want (or at least need) to agree. Progress is stymied unless they admit that agreement is necessary.

Assuming they agree on the conflict's cause and the need to resolve it:

1. *Have each party "blow off steam" (psychologists call this "vent-*

ing") *by summarizing their respective views.* They must follow two absolute rules, however:

—Only one person speaks at a time.

—No personal attacks. Complaints about behavior are fair game as long as they don't cross the line. If behavior is at fault, expect to hear gripes such as "You don't give me the information I need on time," "Your frequent absences make my job harder to do," "You take personal calls and let me do all the work," "You don't seem as worried about meeting deadlines as I am," "I think we can do better, but you seem happy with things the way they are," "You took credit for my work," "You're not carrying your fair share of the load," and "You don't seem to respect my efforts."

> **|Best Tip**
>
> Don't settle disputes. Take on the role of facilitator and mediator and help team members come to an understanding.

2. Have both sides describe what they feel they must have (not what they'd like to have) from the other side to help them and the team do the best possible job.

3. Have each side list at least three things that the other side does well in the relationship. A glass isn't necessarily half empty. It's also half full. Guide them to look for strong points and see each other from positive angles. Steer them away from seeing each other as totally inept. You can usually find some good in most people if you look hard enough. Even the maniac in *The Silence of the Lambs* loved his dog!

4. Don't allow yourself to be conned into arbitrating the dispute. Parties to a conflict sometimes feel more comfortable dumping responsibility for its settlement into someone else's lap. If you let them do that, however, they haven't really reached agreement at all. They're merely accepting—sometimes grudgingly—a third party's decree. Play the role of objective facilitator and mediator and stick to it.

5. Given all the information the steps above have placed on the table, urge the teammates to set a good-faith deadline for resolving their problem and informing the rest of the team of what they intend to do. Don't hesitate to employ peer pressure. This practice can be helpful in one-against-the team situations and one-on-one disputes that handicap the team's productivity. The prospect of group disapproval or sanctions can be a powerful motivator for out-of-synch teammates to revise their attitudes, priorities, or work habits.

Organize Gripe Sessions

Don't wait for conflict to approach the boiling point before taking action. Head off potential trouble by prompting your team to hold periodic gripe sessions that allow teammates to discuss concerns openly and productively.

1. **Call it what it is.** Simply calling the meeting a "gripe session" can be positive because it helps employees who have problems put themselves in the proper frame of mind for the meeting and helps them assemble the information they need to address whatever's been bothering them.

Although you shouldn't dictate the agenda (recall chapter three), you can and sometimes should propose possible topics for discussion, based on how team members have been relating to one another and their work. These may include, for example, job assignments, interpersonal communications and relationships among certain teammates, work habits, and the availability and condition of resources the team needs to do its job.

2. **Use the session to assess the state of your team.** Evaluate comments by individual members. Note signs of morale problems, interpersonal conflicts, and polarized attitudes that may divide the team into opposing factions and dilute its effectiveness. Don't overlook body language!

3. **Reaffirm your support and commitment.** Verify that you'll do everything possible to correct problems, eliminate roadblocks, and secure needed resources. A gripe session can be an excellent place to confirm your role as facilitator.

4. **Consider taking notes.** If team members air gripes about

facilities, equipment, or other resources that may need higher management approval, record details of the meeting. Doing so can be valuable if you have to submit a requisition or make a proposal to higher management.

Best Tip

A great gripe session: When people leave feeling better than when they arrived.

5. Ask for specifics. Guide team members away from generalities like, "We need more support," "The system's a mess," "The red tape's ridiculous." These comments are too vague to act on. Probe for specifics with remarks such as "I need some details," "Give me something tangible to work with," or "Summarize the problem and put it in perspective for me."

6. Ask each team member to contribute something to the session. Official gripe sessions are the best time and place for people to unload. Nobody should leave the room with the same burdens they brought in. You'll sometimes discover that two teammates have been battling identical complaints or problems independently, suffering in silence, and growing more frustrated. A gripe session that brings common problems to light also sets the stage for teammates to join forces and attack them together.

7. Use summary comments that express people's feelings. Remarks such as "You seem to be saying . . . ," "If I understand you correctly . . . ," and "So it's your opinion that . . ." encourage team members to communicate frankly and eliminate any confusion about what they think versus what they said. Summary comments may also prompt others to share their feelings on the matter and contribute additional information.

8. Make a commitment. As chapter three pointed out, meetings need closure. Close a gripe session by outlining your understanding of teammates' conflicts and problems, getting their confirmation, and pledging to do all within your power as team leader to investigate and resolve them. Set a deadline if necessary for informing your team of your progress and follow up.

This puts your reputation on the line and further demonstrates your sincerity and commitment to your team's success.

Deal with Talented Mavericks

OK, let's be honest here. There will probably be some employees, for whatever reasons, who simply refuse to march in your teamwork parade. You can lead those horses to water, but they still refuse to drink. What might you do with hard cases who won't buy into the program?

Assign them to sub-teams whose work complements their interests and skills. They may find that's the best place to let their creativity flow. Meanwhile, they're learning the value of teamwork and compromise in miniature.

Restate the importance of cooperation and team spirit. Leave no doubt that an attitude adjustment may be both necessary and mandatory. People with contradictory feelings can erode team spirit and keep your group in a perpetual state of frustration.

Review the person's background, skills, and experience. Perhaps you can justify transferring a valuable individualist to another posi-

---

Teamwork Triumphs

BASF Corporation has set up a total of thirty self-directed work teams at its Clemson, South Carolina facility. Teammates take turns as team leaders with the goal of working together on a single level instead of in a hierarchy.

Teams are responsible for solving problems with materials flow and quality assurance and planning vacations and shift work. Technical knowledge alone isn't enough to ensure that team activities run smoothly. Although occasionally involved in critical situations, former supervisors mostly serve as moderators and advisors—work that requires them to develop more social skills.

Higher management applauds the teams' spirit of innovation and the critical difference they've made in the company's competitive position.

tion or department where a team-oriented attitude isn't part of the job specification. Ask such questions as:

- Do you realize that we're all expected to buy into team-work in this company? There's really not much choice.
- Do you understand that your negative feelings about working as part of a team could impair your future here?
- What's your main objection to working as part of our team?
- How would you describe the type of job you'd most like to be doing in our organization?
- How do you feel about investing your own time and money to qualify for a position that doesn't require teamwork?

Although these actions may be practical for rare breeds with exotic skills, most employees—especially philosophical mavericks who think the world is out of step with them—shouldn't expect to have their cake and eat it, too.

If you feel some people are trying to manipulate you into crossing the line from accommodation to capitulation, the only cost-effective move may be to let these non-team players go seek their fortune elsewhere. After all, no one is indispensable.

The Agile Manager's Checklist

✔ Watch for friction. It arises from a lack of support for teamwork, satisfaction with the status quo, teammates who are slackers, feelings of inequity, or arguments.
✔ Challenge and rebuild counterproductive attitudes.
✔ Organize gripe sessions to acknowledge the existence of conflicts and help teammates address them positively.
✔ Don't ignore conflicts and hope they'll go away. They won't.
✔ Help valuable employees adapt to teamwork or find a suitable niche. But don't let them take advantage of you.

Chapter Five

Make Brilliant Team Decisions

"[W]ithout [compromise] the world would have come to a standstill. If I cannot have my way and you cannot have yours, perhaps there is a middle ground we can both accept. It is as simple as that, and every day of our lives we are compromising in every possible way, adjusting and adapting to what needs to be done."

LOUIS L'AMOUR
EDUCATION OF A WANDERING MAN

". . . and I honestly couldn't come up with a reason against using plastic housing for it," said Anita, sitting at the head of the conference table. *"It'll save us 18 percent over the cost of metal."*

"Did you check with a major customer?" asked Manuel.

"Two of them. Both said the same thing: As long as it holds up under daily use, it shouldn't matter."

"I don't know," said Manuel. *"Something bothers me about this. It's never been done."*

"If we did only things that have been done before . . ." Anita let her sentence trail off, having made the point.

71

"Will," said Wanda, *"can you give me one good reason why we shouldn't use molded plastic?"*

"Not really," he said. *"And I don't think this is an issue to get excited about, Manuel. The item on next week's agenda about whether to outsource the power supply—that's something we can sink our teeth into."*

"Yeah, you're right," said Manuel. *"Let's go with plastic."*

"Good," said Wanda. *"And about that outsourcing decision: Anita, I don't care how you really feel about the issue. I'd like you to come in against outsourcing and have reasons ready to fire at us . . ."*

It's an understatement to say that team decisions are important. In today's team-based organizations, teams routinely make (or at least influence) decisions that not only affect the operations of the team itself but also the operations of "customer" departments, related teams in other areas, and the entire company.

Team decision making may be the ultimate collaborative effort. And rightly so. Inept managers may contend that too many cooks spoil the broth. Agile managers and their teammates, however, realize that collective decisions have the potential to produce a gourmet banquet of creativity that makes unilateral decisions about as tasty as a cardboard pizza.

Use the Right Type of Decision

Your team may first have to decide what kind of decision is best for the situation:

Consensus. Consensus decisions are important when the situation requires unified support and synchronized effort. It's sort of like building a pyramid. If just one person's contribution is out of place or missing, the whole project's going to suffer. (Never mind that the pyramids in Egypt were built by slaves—who did a good deal of suffering no matter how team-oriented they were.)

Consensus decisions can take an awful lot of time, and time can be scarce when a crisis is about to kick in your office door and attack you. But on the plus side, they tend to ensure that every member of your team officially buys into the agreement.

It's often mentioned that Japanese management styles are big on consensus and unanimity. So much so, in fact, that all the people involved in a key decision may be asked to sign off on a written summary of it to affirm their acceptance and symbolize their commitment. This process reduces the odds that some people will drag their heels secretly.

Consensus is important when everybody's got to give 110 percent to make the decision work. Consensus might be preferred, for example, if a team is supposed to reduce new product design-to-market time by 60 percent, reorganize a department's physical layout for maximum efficiency, or set objectives for the next fiscal year.

Best Tip

Make consensus decisions when the situation requires all team members to agree on and work toward the solution.

Majority vote. This is often the most practical way to make a decision, especially when time is short, the decision isn't critical, and you don't need universal agreement.

For example, a team may decide by majority vote how to prioritize current projects or budget expenditures, which word processing or spreadsheet program to adopt, how long to retain hard-copy files before placing them in an archive facility, and what vacation and shift schedules team members will follow for the next work period.

Team appointee. This is the designated-driver version of decisions. The team nominates one person who'll be responsible for calling the shots. Choosing the appointee will require a consensus or majority decision, of course, but once that's out of the way, the appointee can move faster than the group.

An appointee may be chosen to pick the location for an off-site conference, arrange for a guest speaker at the monthly team pep rally, do a preliminary evaluation of new hardware, software, or equipment that the department might buy, negotiate with vendors to buy standard materials, parts, and support services up to a specified amount, or hire a freelance graphic artist to illustrate a new product brochure.

Deal with Naysayers

Dissenters and devil's advocates are necessary to any team. They can provide a healthy balance by challenging the team's direction and perhaps keeping everyone from charging, lemming-like, over a cliff.

The trouble is, naysayers can also be disruptive and polarizing. There are some people—no doubt you've worked with them—who revel in stirring up trouble just for the hell of it. There's even a type of Middle Eastern bread whose name describes them: PITA. (The *P* stands for *pain*. You figure out the rest.)

If your team has one or more folks who have inherited the PITA gene, you'll be challenged to channel their personalities and attitudes constructively. While you don't want to destroy their participation and input—which can sometimes be valuable—they can't be allowed to monopolize or dominate your team's decision-making process. What might you do?

- Recognize their contribution. ("Thank you for your input, Dean. We need to know how each of us feels about this, and you've left no doubt where you stand.")
- Try to break their grip on discussion by asking them to acknowledge at least one *positive* aspect of the issue or decision they seem bent on torpedoing. ("Jean, we see your point, but would you try to look at this a little more objectively? I'm sure you're sharp enough to see at least one or two advantages, too. Tell us what they are.")
- Summarize and put in perspective their background and experience. ("Tim, your twenty-two years as a military officer make you a valued member of our team. You have some unique views. But we need to talk about some civilian solutions to this problem, too.")
- Don't allow them to disagree disagreeably. Invoke your team's operating rules if necessary to prohibit shouting matches and personal attacks on teammates who take opposing views.

Steps to a Decision

The process of making team decisions parallels the process for making any management decision. The big difference is that the process is being used by a group instead of one person.

1. Define the problem. The team should use Kipling's "six good serving men"—what, where, when, how, why, and who.

In addition, don't be blinded by symptoms of what's really wrong. For example, a batch of defective products on a production line could be caused by inadequate training, defective materials, machines that were out of adjustment, miscalibrated manufacturing or quality-assurance equipment, sabotage by disgruntled workers, or any combination thereof.

Attacking symptoms instead of problems is a critical and expensive mistake. Here are a couple of examples—one embarrassing and one profitable—from yours truly.

- I came home one day and found that my garage door opener wouldn't work. The remote control had been acting up for several weeks, and this malfunction was the last straw. I got out of the car and flung it down on the driveway. Transistors, batteries, and miscellaneous other electronic parts flew every which way. When I unlocked the front door and turned on the light switch, I made an interesting discovery. The electricity was off in the house!

- In 1993 I decided to look for an older sports car to restore, a car that would be a nostalgic daily driver and a fun hobby as well. An acquaintance had a 1976 Datsun 280-Z that he wanted to sell.

   The body had minor sideswipe damage and the paint was a mess, but the drive train was in great condition. "This car has a terrible electrical problem, though," he warned. "It'll probably cost a fortune to fix." One headlight went dim and shut off within a minute of being turned on, the dash lights flashed intermittently, and the turn signals seemed possessed by demons.

Realizing that these were symptoms and not problems, I bought the car for $450 and took it to an auto electric repair shop I had used for several years. They found the problem in fifteen minutes. Someone had wired a trailer light kit to the taillights incorrectly, which produced all the crazy symptoms. The technician simply disconnected the light kit and charged just $15 labor for diagnosing what was wrong.

It's also helpful to label or categorize a problem when you define it. Is it a process problem? A procedural problem? A people problem (behavior, performance, or both)? A team or subgroup problem? A situation that must be resolved? Putting a frame around it helps your team visualize and relate to it better.

At the end of the definition and framing process, you may want to describe the problem in writing. This practice is especially important if the decision's going to be made by consensus. If the team can't agree on the problem's definition, how can they hope to agree on a common solution?

One of my favorite techniques is to ask team members to write out their personal definitions of what's wrong in private, then meet to discuss each one, get clarification and details if necessary, reconsider their definitions, and generate a group definition that's acceptable to all.

Best Tip

Dig deep when assessing a problem. Symptoms often hide the real one.

It's also important to identify "outsiders" such as other internal or external teams, customers, vendors, regulatory agencies, and competitors who may have an influence on, or can give your team some meaningful input to, its decision. Your team may need to meet with such groups to get added objectivity and information. Realizing this now can save lots of backtracking and frustration later.

2. Research potential solutions. Chapter three's brainstorming suggestions certainly apply here. So can your team's ability to accept uncertainty and ambiguity. They'll virtually never have enough time to gather all the information they need, and lots of solutions will appear in shades of gray.

Outside forces and powers beyond the team's control also impose limitations. A retired Navy captain once told me, "Every decision has three considerations: What you *should* do, what you *can* do, and what you eventually *will* do. They're not always one and the same." Good point. The team's ultimate decision will have to take into account a host of conditions, including:

- Limited resources (money, time, space, equipment, and skills).
- Policies and procedures (if your team's not empowered to change 'em, it will have to live with 'em).
- Higher management attitudes. Your team will have to go with the flow. Even a team of synchronized swimmers can drown in a riptide.

This solution-generating step doesn't have to involve the whole team. Sometimes it's more practical to break into sub-teams and have each one investigate a different potential solution or delve into certain aspects of a favored one.

3. Let things incubate. If at all possible, set aside time so that team members can put the whole matter on their mental back burners and let it simmer for a while.

If nothing else, contemplation helps the team avoid making snap judgments or forgetting to examine most of the angles. At best, a little incubating may produce a clearer definition of the problem, generate new ideas about how to tackle it, reveal concerns you hadn't thought of earlier, help you prioritize your list of possible actions better, or see how the favored solution might be tweaked and polished to make it work better.

Although I wasn't there at the time, legend has it that Archimedes, who was asked to determine the alloy content in a gold crown without destroying the crown, incubated the situation for a number of days. A suitable technique finally came to him while he was taking a bath, and he dashed nude through the streets shouting, "Eureka!" (I've found it!)

4. Pilot run or pretest the most "doable" solution. A pilot run can:

- Help you debug the solution by identifying potential difficulties that weren't obvious at first glance.
- Get feedback from other teams and individuals who may be involved in implementing the solution.
- Clarify each team member's responsibilities if the team decides to go full-speed ahead.
- Protect your team's reputation. If top management is watching the situation closely, a pilot run can either (a) confirm the idea's soundness and support your request for more funding from On High or (b) confirm that the idea, which may have sounded great on paper, would be a disaster in practice. You could cut your losses, abandon the whole thing, and start over without having bet the rent.

5. Commit to it. Backed by confirmation from your pilot run, your team can implement the surviving solution, following up with adjustments as necessary for situations or factors that may not have surfaced during the pilot run.

Let's see how this all comes together. One of the textile plants I worked in formed a quality-improvement team of representatives from production, quality assurance, human resources, and maintenance. The team was responsible for raising quality to the same level as the benchmark plant in the division.

The key question was, what caused the discrepancy in quality? Team members visited the leading plant, interviewed their counterparts there, took notes, and went back to examine their own facility.

One major difference surfaced between the two plants: lighting fixtures in the production area. The top-performing plant's fixtures were newer and somewhat brighter. But did that really cause the quality discrepancy? The team realized that employee training, equipment maintenance, and certain other factors might be at fault. After exploring each of these possibilities and finding no significant differences, the team decided that lighting was probably the culprit.

Buying all new light fixtures for the production area would

cost thousands of dollars, however, and the team wasn't willing to risk such an investment without a pilot run. They bought two dozen new fixtures, installed them above specific looms, and monitored the quality of the products that came off those machines. After several weeks, it was obvious that the better-lit machines produced superior goods. This fact led the team to do a cost/benefit analysis, which justified the expense to install new light fixtures throughout the production department.

A Word About Opportunities

Although the process just described was related to solving problems, don't overlook its value when dealing with opportunities, too. Just include these ideas.

Analyze costs and benefits and calculate the opportunity cost. You'll need to figure the estimated payoff before you can convince higher management to hand over the resources (especially money) your team will need.

Evaluate your teammates' readiness. Do they have the necessary skills? If not, how long will it take to acquire them? Is training available? If not, should you recruit team members who possess the desired skills already?

What resources do you need to assemble? Which team members are best able to acquire them? (Deciding may fall to you, their leader!)

Weigh the team's collective feeling. Does everyone support the new venture? If not, will you need a consensus in order to make it succeed? Would a few dissenters jeopardize success?

Work out a timetable for developing and coordinating a plan of attack.

Determine the necessary interaction with other departments and teams both inside and outside your organization. Recalling chapter two, what boundaries must you span?

Make sure this is a legitimate opportunity. Although Henry J. Kaiser said "Problems are opportunities in work clothes," Murphy's Law says, "Inside every major problem are lots of minor problems struggling to get out." Good point.

Some seemingly marvelous ideas have turned out to be—or

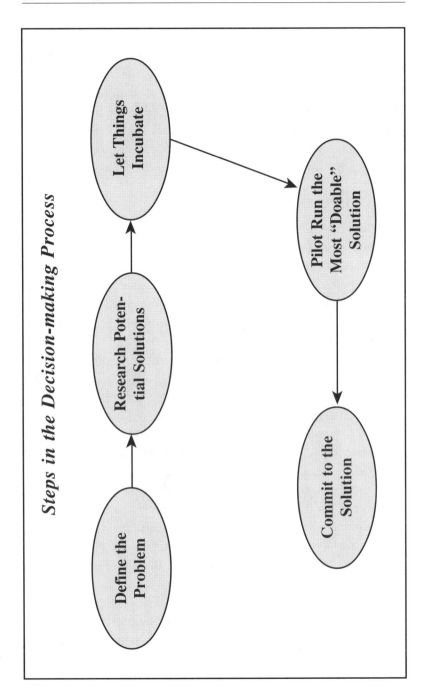

Steps in the Decision-making Process

to generate—massive headaches. For example, one well-intentioned welfare agency got a grant to provide financial assistance to low-income families whose apartments caught fire. The result—as you've likely guessed—is that tenement fires more than doubled after the program was announced.

Watch Out for Groupthink

Remember those old-fashioned shoot-'em-up Westerns where a crowd of intellectually disadvantaged citizenry gathers outside the jail muttering, scratching themselves in private places, waving a rope, and finally screaming, "Get 'im, boys! Let's string him up!"?

That same mob-rule attitude—it's called groupthink—can invade your company. If you're lucky, though, your teammates will smell a little better and at least clean up after their horses.

Groupthink is a virus that can contaminate your team's decision-making process and doom you to mediocrity or worse. It comes in several varieties.

Self-censorship. This is the basis for that fairy tale about the emperor's new clothes. It's the tendency for some teammates to keep unpopular opinions to themselves. Why? Because they're afraid of not fitting in, being branded as a non-team player, upsetting the group's chemistry, dampening its high spirits, or making themselves outcasts by speaking the unthinkable—even though their opinions could give a high-flying team that's about to crash and burn a much-needed reality check.

Selective perception. When a team is on a roll, members sometimes accept or acknowledge only information that confirms its success or reinforces its actions. They filter out, reject, or ignore contradictory data in a misguided effort to protect the team's unanimity and collective psyche.

Selective perceivers sometimes challenge the source, credibility, relevance, or other aspects of information that threatens their peace of mind when in fact they should give it serious consideration. Their battle cry might be, "Our minds are made up. Don't confuse us with the facts." This attitude compares to that of a doting parent at graduation who wonders, "Why is everyone out of step with Michael?"

Peer pressure. Pressure to conform, get in line, not rock the boat, and be "one of the gang" can have the force of an anvil dropped from a 10th-floor window. It shows up each election year in the often-quoted advice to new legislators: "To get along, go along."

It takes guts to challenge actions, proposals, or opinions. Few people are willing to be lightning rods for teammates with opposing views, especially if those teammates outrank them. Those who do often become as popular as a Band-Aid in a punch bowl. The alternative, however, can be deadly.

I once saw a flight training video that used dialogue from the cockpit voice recorder of a crashed airliner. The film dramatized the catastrophic potential of peer pressure in the cockpit. As they approached the airport, the self-assured captain disregarded a series of altitude, speed, and flight-path warnings from anxious crew members whose comments were prefaced with such phrases as "Have you noticed . . .", "Don't you think that . . .", and "We seem to be . . ." The captain even cracked a joke: "What's the difference between a copilot and a duck? A duck can fly."

The instruments continued to report their perilous situation, and the crew's comments took on a more strident tone. By the time the shrieking altitude alarm confirmed the seriousness of their condition, it was too late. Everyone on board was killed because subordinate crew members, concerned about their careers and the captain's wrath, didn't declare in no uncertain terms that they were afraid they were going to crash.

Interpreting silence as agreement. This is typically what happens to self-censors. Because they don't overtly object, teammates may assume that they agree when in fact they don't—and often for good reason. It's important to have all team members go on record and vocalize their position.

Invincibility. This attitude sometimes accounts for major upsets and embarrassment on the gridiron. For example, LSU and

Teamwork Triumphs

Beginning in 1992, employees and managers at AT&T Corporation's Atlanta Service Center reorganized their jobs and work flow around self-directed work teams of some five to twenty members. All have been pleased with the results.

Under this new system, team leaders coordinate personnel movements and work closely with production and performance managers on a daily basis. Teams are empowered to change work processes as they see fit and coordinate across boundaries if changes in one process affect other teams or areas. In addition, leaders balance work and manpower loads by meeting regularly to see if they either need or can supply temporary help from their teams as the case may be. Teams decide their own education and training needs.

Speaking of education, a self-directed Education Team provides interpersonal and personal skills training, identifies necessary changes in training modules, and works with a Training Team to redesign training. Composed of employees from the shop floor, Education Team members are trained in train-the-trainer courses.

Employees at this facility receive wide-ranging, intensive training that includes more than thirty hours of formal classroom training each year. A Methods Team provides training to employees when they move between teams.

Thanks to self-directed work teams, AT&T's Atlanta Service Center has been able to flatten its already-flat management hierarchy even more. Before switching to teamwork, the Center had just three levels of management. Supervisors were eliminated entirely through attrition after the team-based system was installed, and team leaders and coordinators now perform their tasks.

University of Georgia fans were delighted to see their teams thrash higher-ranked University of Florida and send its conference and national championship hopes down the drain in 1997.

Invincibility is self-deception. An arrogant "Can't nothin' beat us" slogan might better be replaced with, "If everything seems to be going well, we've probably overlooked something."

Combat Groupthink

Now let's polish your suit of armor, saddle your horse, and prepare to do battle with groupthink. You have several weapons to choose from.

1. Appoint a gadfly or devil's advocate. When it comes to advocating devil's advocates, we've been there/done that back in chapter three. Let's say here, though, that gadflies are handy folks to have on your team when it comes to giving complacency and cookie-cutter thinking the boot. Consider rotating the role so nobody gets stereotyped as a professional PITA.

2. Practice round-robin questioning. This is an orchestrated version of the gadfly technique, and you're the orchestra conductor. If you're worried that groupthink may have cast its spell on your team, causing it to act like one big happy family, go around the room and ask each team member such questions as:

- What makes you uncomfortable with this idea?
- On a scale of 1 to 10, how certain are you that this is the best solution?
- How would you criticize this idea if someone held a gun to your head and ordered you to? (Note: Don't use this line if you're a team leader for the U.S. Postal Service.)

3. Use NGT (Nominal Group Technique). NGT can wipe out groupthink by dispersing the group. It works like this:

- Once your team has agreed on a definition of the problem, have them adjourn and write down their private thoughts about how to solve it.
- Reconvene and ask each person to present his or her ideas to the group *with no feedback or comments allowed.* Nobody else talks; everybody listens.
- Open the floor for group discussion. Teammates can pro-

vide details about their ideas if anybody wants more.

■ Have teammates rank the proposed solutions independently from most- to least-favored.

■ Compare the individual rankings. The solution that gets the most first-place votes wins.

4. Use the essay technique. This might be called the office version of "How I Spent My Summer Vacation." Ask teammates to submit and justify their proposed solutions in, say, 1,000 words or less.

While this exercise shouldn't be done too often (it takes time away from more pressing obligations), it forces people to marshal and clarify their thoughts, examine and challenge assumptions, and prepare cogent arguments for their favored solutions.

The essay technique is almost guaranteed to produce more and better information than if everyone just sat around a conference table firing off words into thin air. And if the solution the team finally picks needs higher management's approval, much of the boilerplate language, number crunching, and other grunt work needed for the proposal has already been done.

The Agile Manager's Checklist

✔ Depending on the situation, make decisions by consensus, majority, or team appointee.

✔ Follow a five-step decision-making process:

■ Define the problem.

■ Research potential solutions.

■ Let things incubate.

■ Pilot run the most "doable" solution.

■ Commit to it.

✔ Prepare to do battle with all forms of groupthink. It destroys honest dialogue and creative ideas.

Chapter Six

*E*valuate Team Performance Fairly

"TEAM = Together Everyone Achieves More."

"And the boss was so happy you beat the deadline by three weeks and met all the quality standards that he gave me $25,000 to parcel out," said the Agile Manager. The Product Development Action Team hooted and slapped each other's hands.

"Of course, I'm not going to do that," said the Agile Manager. People looked at him quizzically. "Here Wanda," he said handing her the authorization. "You and your team divide it as you see fit."

"Yet more responsibility," said Anita.

"That's what it's all about," said the Agile Manager. "You take responsibility for results, and you get rewarded accordingly. And each according to the contribution made, I hope."

Thanks a lot for that last comment, thought Wanda.

"Hey—let's make it easy," said Jim. "Let's just decide to divide it evenly now." He smiled.

Everyone else looked at Jim and thought exactly the same thing: You contributed the least of anyone.

Manuel was thinking, I probably deserve more than anyone except Anita. I wonder if I'll get it.

Anita was thinking, I'd like to divide it equally, except for Jim.
Will was thinking, Phil and I did the lion's share of the work, but
Anita came through at key times. Wanda, too . . .
Wanda surveyed the scene and had an idea what each was
thinking. Team challenges never end, do they? she thought. "Hey
everybody? I can see your thoughts and I don't like them. This
process can't be subjective. We have to hash it out fairly, just as
we did when we made each key decision on the 3600A. Now
remember that each of us has had quantifiable standards to meet,
and we did peer reviews only last month. What I suggest is . . ."

Who evaluates team performance? That depends on which
type of team you are. Troubleshooting or advisory teams (see
chapter one), which have minimal autonomy, might be evaluated by one or more higher managers. At the other end of the
scale, self-directed teams have evolved to the point where they
may evaluate themselves.

Higher management generally provides overall direction and
sets the basic ground rules that govern how the team operates.
Senior managers would therefore be the people to clarify the
team's collective responsibility and accountability and how its
achievements will be gauged.

Whatever the case, both team and individual performance
should be evaluated, since they're interdependent. The team's
fate is largely decided by the quality of each member's efforts.
(Hardly a surprise, eh?) Teammates who share camaraderie and
work in harmony accomplish infinitely more than what they
could achieve individually. That's synergy's finest hour.

Teammates who don't meet their obligations to the team,
however, jeopardize the performance, unity, and perhaps the very
existence of the entire group.

Set Performance Standards

Most performance standards that apply to individual workers
can be applied to a team too. Here are a few basic guidelines for
setting those standards:

Involve all team members in setting performance standards. This is especially critical if you're leading a high-autonomy team. Members who aren't included in setting performance standards often resent being excluded from the process. They'll perceive they were railroaded or dictated to by their teammates.

An unwilling horse runs a reluctant race. Likewise, higher managers who impose goals on a team autocratically or arbitrarily, without the team's active participation, should expect grudging support at best.

Make standards realistic and challenging. They should be realistic, because it's crazy to expect a team to fly to the moon on a bottle rocket. Standards should also be challenging, however, because teams and their individual members should be expected to stretch beyond previous limits, break new ground, master and apply new skills, and surpass their former achievements. Challenge is the core of excellence and the essence of progress. People without challenge are like swimmers treading water. They burn lots of energy and make plenty of waves, but they're going nowhere.

|Best Tip

Set challenging—and measurable—standards. It's the only way you and the team will grow and improve.

Quantify standards. Numerical benchmarks are usually possible and often ideal. They can be measured objectively; there's no doubt whether they've been met.

Quantified performance standards might include, for example, response time on customer service requests; performance in excess of last month's goals; number of customer complaints received during the month; reductions in waste, scrap, or rework; quantity of products produced or services performed; the volume or dollar value of supplies and other resources consumed; absences caused by personal illness (especially on Monday or Friday); hours of overtime or weekend work done voluntarily; number of ideas submitted to the employee/team suggestion

Teamwork Triumphs

In speaking to his troops, Brigadier General Joseph Cannady of the North Carolina Air National Guard emphasized the valuable teamwork lessons to be learned from a flock of geese flying in formation.

1. As each bird flaps its wings, it creates an uplift for the one behind it. A flock flying in a "V" formation can travel 71 percent farther than one goose can alone. (Employees with a common direction and unified purpose can get where they're going faster and easier by supporting each other.)

2. Geese who fall out of formation feel the drag and resistance of flying alone. They rejoin the formation to take advantage of the lift of the bird immediately in front. (Employees are better off staying in formation with those who are heading where they want to go.)

3. When the lead goose gets tired, it drops back and lets another goose take over. (Teammates depend on each other. They should be willing to surrender or assume the lead when necessary.)

4. Rear members of the flock honk to encourage those up front to maintain their speed. (Teammates should encourage one another.)

5. If a goose becomes sick or injured, two others drop out of formation, follow it down, and help and protect it. They stay until it flies or dies, then they catch up with their own flock or rejoin another. (Teammates should stand by each other in bad times as well as good.)

Teammates, like geese, should realize the benefits of flying in formation.

program; and courses and seminars teammates have completed on their own time or at their own expense.

Communicate and demonstrate performance standards to everyone. All team members must have both oars in the water and pull in the same direction.

Keep standards flexible, and review them during the work period. If business conditions change for the better, raise performance standards to acknowledge that fact. If business takes a dip, it makes sense to consider lowering standards a notch or two. (Yes, management rarely does that—but does it make sense to hold a team to a level of performance that an abrupt economic decline or a major strategy shift by competitors has made virtually impossible?)

What should standards address? All the traditional areas and some team-oriented ones, too. These include:

- The quality of the product or service that the team's supposed to deliver.
- Intrateam and interteam cooperation. Do teammates support each other voluntarily? Do they cooperate fully with peer teams inside the organization and counterparts at suppliers' and customers' firms?
- Customer satisfaction. This is everyone's job. Is the team totally committed to doing it well?
- Process improvements. Are team members actively dedicated to finding a better way? Do they voluntarily challenge the status quo in pursuit of superior methods and techniques?
- Problem-solving. How well does the team function as a problem-solving unit? Do members respond objectively and collectively to help things get back on track, regardless of who's at fault?
- Skill development. Are team members mutually supportive and enthusiastic about cultivating and refining their respective skills, cross-training one another, and nurturing each other's personal growth and development within the team?

Create Feedback Channels

Setting quantified performance criteria is only part of the job, of course. It's also necessary to create feedback channels that confirm how well teams and teammates meet those criteria. The more feedback channels you have, the more thoroughly you're equipped to assess team performance objectively. Here are six of them, along with some suggestions about how they could be applied.

1. Higher manager review. If a team reports to a higher executive (as opposed to being self-directed), that manager must look and listen, mix and mingle, and stay close to the team without meddling or becoming a nuisance. He or she must thoroughly grasp the performance of the group and understand the contributions of each member. Absentee or haphazard evaluators do teams an enormous injustice.

Best Tip

Get feedback from every group your team works with. The more feedback channels, the more objective the evaluation.

2. Team leader committee review. Leaders may meet periodically as a team evaluation committee to assess the performance of their teams relative to each other. This gives them an opportunity to discuss coordination and cooperation problems among the teams as a whole and address conflicts that may have surfaced between members of individual teams.

3. Team leader feedback. Agile managers give their teammates frequent feedback about progress toward performance goals throughout the work period.

Use charts, graphs, and other visual aids to summarize the performance of individuals and the entire team. Don't post this information as a "management by embarrassment" tactic, however. Negative publicity makes a team the butt of humiliation and ridicule.

Part of your job as a feedback provider should be to create communications channels between your team and the other teams, groups, and individuals they communicate with.

- Arrange tours of suppliers' and customers' facilities so your team can log valuable "face time" with people they've been dealing with at arm's length. On the flip side, arranging for suppliers' and customers' teams to visit your office or plant helps them understand your company's operations better.

- Hold brainstorming sessions between your team and the internal and external teams they work with routinely. This gives them an opportunity to propose and discuss solutions to quality, service, coordination, and information-exchange problems that may be blocking superior performance.
- Arrange meetings between your team and the major non-team "customers" it serves—production workers, the sales staff, and customer service personnel, for example. Such feedback confirms the performance of your team.
- Celebrate your team's success with the world. Post customer compliments, higher management praise, and outstanding performance records on a bulletin board.

4. Peer evaluations. Self-directed work teams often evaluate their own performance. How effectively they do this is an index not only of their effectiveness as a team but also of their ability to work together with minimal outside influence and control. Peer pressure tends to bring slackers up to speed if a team's compensation is decreased by the actions of a few who aren't pulling their weight. Some criteria for peer evaluations:

—Do teammates set self-challenging goals for performance and personal development that require them to stretch beyond the last work period's achievements?

—Do some teammates have hidden personal agendas that overshadow or undermine their relationships with teammates and the work of the team itself?

—Are any members preoccupied with interpersonal conflicts (recall chapter four) that are diverting their attention and draining their energy away from achieving the team's collective goals?

Teammates don't necessarily have to evaluate peers on their own teams, of course. They can also evaluate members of other teams. At AT&T, for example, self-directed work teams have eliminated the need for supervisors to monitor customer services at many offices. Instead, a monitoring team of about eight to ten employees—sometimes called a "customer delight team"—decides the best way to monitor calls in a particular office.

Members serve for approximately twelve months.

Operators are evaluated against eight quality criteria including courtesy, helpfulness, and knowledge. To build in objectivity, monitoring teams evaluate the work of customer service operators in other service centers instead of their own.

5. *Customer evaluations.* In addition to creating the somewhat informal customer feedback channels recommended above, it's important to consider using more formal sources to gather customers' opinions about team performance. These might consist of:

- Focus groups
- Gripe sessions
- Customer complaint letters and transcribed accounts of oral complaints made by phone or in person
- Unsolicited written or oral compliments
- Customer-response cards enclosed with invoices
- Mail and telephone surveys conducted with appropriate individuals and teams.

6. *Outside vendors.* Vendors' employees, like internal and external customers, are in an excellent position to assess the quality of your team's performance.

Compensate Team Members Fairly

Teamwork's popularity has posed some challenges when it comes to compensation methods. No company has created the ideal way to acknowledge and reward individuals for their contributions to group goals.

Fortunately, there's general agreement about what team-based pay systems should do:

1. Encourage and reward above-average group performance.

2. Motivate team members to maintain, and preferably exceed, previous levels of performance.

3. Minimize lag time. Team members should be paid for success as soon as possible to keep their enthusiasm and commitment at its peak.

4. Show a direct link between results and rewards.

Teamwork Triumphs

Kraft Foods, a subsidiary of Philip Morris Companies, Inc., is dedicated to improving every step in the consumer value chain from purchasing raw materials through manufacturing and marketing. Teamwork makes that happen.

■ Manufacturing teams work continuously to improve quality and reduce costs.

■ Cross-functional marketing teams develop brand and business strategies to compete in the marketplace. There's even a team responsible for developing new products for children. Marketing teams also conduct brand research and provide advertising, promotion, and other support services.

■ A sales force of 300 customer business teams operating in twenty-one regions creates retail sales and provides service to Kraft's retailers nationwide.

■ Teams include staff employees from finance, information systems, human resources, corporate strategy, corporate affairs, and the legal department. They have input to decisions in all major areas.

---

5. Compensate performance objectively based on quantitative measures whenever possible.

6. Include input from team members when deciding on performance goals, frequency of compensation, performance evaluation methods, and ways to ensure that compensation is commensurate with performance.

7. Build in challenges that motivate employees to reach beyond their present levels of performance.

8. Include a base rate for all team members and an incentive rate that rewards individual efforts and contributions to the team's success in such areas as customer satisfaction, increased productivity and efficiency, and cost savings.

9. Allow team members to share the financial rewards of cost-saving measures they've proposed and implemented.

Companies are reluctant to let teams design and administer their own compensation systems. It's too much like letting the cat guard the cream. So the overall team compensation method is usually created by top management in a non-collaborative (OK, unilateral) fashion.

There are at least four alternative techniques, however.

Group pay for performance. This approach evaluates and rewards comprehensive team performance. It may give little attention to the contributions of individual team members. This can cause disputes among teammates when some believe that others haven't pulled their weight or that their skills are more valuable or their contributions more significant than those of certain co-workers.

Pay for knowledge. This method can motivate individual team members to expand the inventory of skills they bring to the team's table. However, the company must have a reliable way to assess each employee's skill set and level of mastery.

Pay for cost-saving suggestions. This share-the-wealth approach motivates teams to watch the bottom line and produce innovative cost-saving suggestions in their respective areas. It promotes cost-consciousness throughout the organization and encourages employee participation.

Group bonus. This method rewards teams for achieving their objectives on or ahead of schedule and under budget.

The Agile Manager's Checklist

✔ Set performance standards that are:
  - Produced with input from all team members.
  - Realistic and challenging.
  - Quantified.
  - Communicated and demonstrated to everyone.
  - Flexible and subject to review.
✔ Apply standards to quality, cooperation, customer satisfaction, process improvements, problem solving, and skill development.